The Unknown Science Of Dark Psychology

Master the Secrets and Techniques of Dark Human Behavior, Persuasion, Psychological Warfare, Brainwashing, NLP, Deception, Mind Manipulation, Hypnotism, and Seduction

Kyle Murphy

© Copyright 2019 - All rights reserved.

The content contained within this book may not be reproduced, duplicated or transmitted without direct written permission from the author or the publisher.

Under no circumstances will any blame or legal responsibility be held against the publisher, or author, for any damages, reparation, or monetary loss due to the information contained within this book. Either directly or indirectly.

Legal Notice:

This book is copyright protected. This book is only for personal use. You cannot amend, distribute, sell, use, quote or paraphrase any part, or the content within this book, without the consent of the author or publisher.

Disclaimer Notice:

Please note the information contained within this document is for educational and entertainment purposes only. All effort has been executed to present accurate, up to date, and reliable, complete information. No warranties of any kind are declared or implied. Readers acknowledge that the author is not engaging in the rendering of legal, financial, medical or professional advice. The content within this book has been derived from various sources. Please consult a licensed professional before attempting any techniques outlined in this book.

By reading this document, the reader agrees that under no circumstances is the author responsible for any losses, direct or indirect, which are incurred as a result of the use of information contained within this document, including, but not limited to, — errors, omissions, or inaccuracies.

Contents

Introduction 1

What Is Dark Psychology 3

Dark Psychology Defined 3

What Is a Dark Personality? 5

How Do People Develop a Dark Personality? 9

The Dark Triad 12

How to Identify Each Individual 14

The Dirty Dozen Test 25

The Power of Persuasion 31

The Techniques of Persuasion 32

The Fine Line between Manipulation and Persuasion 38

How to Persuade People 42

Undetectable Mind Control 51

How to Tell if You Are Being Mind-Controlled .. 52

How to Use Mind Control on People 59

How to Analyze Someone 61

Covert Emotional Manipulation 69

Techniques of Manipulation 69

Characteristics of a Manipulator 77

How to Outsmart a Manipulator 80

Brainwashing 84

How Brainwashing Works 85

How You Can be Brainwashed 93

Dark Psychology and Brainwashing 98

Neuro-linguistic Programming: The Basics 104

How Does NLP Work 105

Techniques Surrounding NLP 106

The Fine Art of Deception 110

Why We Lie 112

Deception techniques 117

How to be of Deceptive at Work 119

Hypnotism Utilization 122

The Four Stages of Hypnosis 122

How Does Hypnosis Work 125

How to Hypnotize Someone 127

Dark Seduction Psychology 136

The Techniques Used in Dark Seduction 137

Why People Use Seduction 144

Psychological Warfare 147

Techniques and Methods 149

Case Studies 152

Conclusion 165

Introduction

In a world where we are surrounded by darkness and troublesome people, we have become eager to learn why such people act in certain ways, and endure such a dark mentality. The secret to unlocking power and influence in society revolves around this topic. People who usually practice dark psychology do not often understand it, but for the few who do, will possess the power to get what they want in life in a malicious way, often leaving others powerless. This guide will help you understand and master many different aspects of dark psychology such as: The secrets of dark human behavior, the dark triad, emotional manipulation, hypnotism, NLP, dark seduction psychology, psychological warfare, deception, brainwashing, persuasion, and undetected mind control.

We are going to create light in this darkness by clearly elaborating on the hidden secrets of dark psychology. In case you are interested in knowing the techniques of dark psychology and their application, this book is all you need. Knowledge is always power, and people who access this information can make informed choices to do good or bad for themselves or someone else. You can choose to have the world at your fingertips the right way or the wrong way, as this book addresses both.

You are going to learn the dark art that can take you into the very depth of unexplored worlds, and go from virgin skin, to a master in disguise in just a matter of time. This guide is for the bold and macho who want to unleash their true potential and are tired of getting shackled back by a world of secrets. It is also for the weak minded to gain control and watch for the signs and gain insight on how you choose to live your life.

Chapter 1
WHAT IS DARK PSYCHOLOGY

Dark psychology is a human condition amongst people who prey on the misfortunate events of other people and their lives. Every human on this earth has the potential to victimize others, but many restrain the behavior to act on the impulse. These criminals know no emotion, have no remorse, and lack instinctual drives in social activity.

Dark Psychology Defined

Dark psychology assumes that all humanity has malicious intent toward others, ranging from mild to extreme. Extreme behavioral intentions consist of pure psychopathic thoughts and actions without any coherent ability to know otherwise. Mild behavioral intents include dark thoughts and plans that get pushed aside resulting in the person just being "normal" or a part of society.

Everyone has a dark side, and we are all capable of thinking and doing the worst—what others might classify as dark and evil. Dark psychology represents this fact as a mindset in humanity. Some people try to ignore it, and others embrace it. A dark human may believe and act "evil" because they want to gain power, money, sex, vengeance, or any other selfish purpose. Some people hurt others because it satisfies and pleases them, meaning, they commit horrible acts without objective and have no goal or determination to make them do so.

Dark psychology suggests that everyone has the potential to act brutally. This manner has access to our thoughts, feelings, and perceptions. As one would think or hope that these thoughts were nonexistent, the few people that embrace these thoughts act on them. This is called dark psychology—the few who act impulsively to their dark thoughts and use techniques against the ones who don't.

What Is a Dark Personality?

Someone that has a dark personality will have less empathy then others will. To define what being a dark character means is to develop traits that you would see in a sociopath. To have a dark temperament means to do intentional devilish things to someone or something. A person that consists of having a blackened persona will act and think in inhumane ways without thinking twice about it to gain satisfaction for themselves.

The more in-depth definition is "having developed traits or aspects of those like a narcissist, psychopath, and Machiavellian." This is known as the dark triad, which we will explain in the next chapter. Let's dive a little deeper and explore the signs of if someone were to have a dark personality:

- **Manipulation**

It means to skillfully master your words in making the victim do as you please without them knowing you are doing it. Flattery is an excellent way to manipulate someone. It means to boost someone's confidence and prey on their low self-esteem to get the victim to do as he or she pleases.

- **Moral Lacking**

They are unremorseful when they hurt you. They may say sorry, but only for you to believe they are sorry when they aren't, known as a strategy and technique they use to have you continue to be their victim. In addition to this, once you are down, they will further upset you by making unthoughtful cynical remarks.

Cynicism

They motivate by self-interest and skepticism. They do not trust that people are genuine and sincere. The dark person will show signs of achieving their selfish intents no matter the consequences and feel no obligation to fulfill their intentions in a mannerly way. This can also be classified as egoism.

- **Narcissism**

This means when people become all about themselves. They have an extremely high self-absorption and tend to need lots of attention. If not given the attention, they will succumb to malicious behavior and manipulating you into thinking it's your fault.

- **Psychological Entitlement**

This means they think they are better than others. They see themselves as more than someone else, and no one is equal. If they see that someone is or has better, they pinpoint them as their victim, and use "fake feelings" or whatever they need to do to knock their victim down a notch or two.

- **Psychopathy**

This happens when the person has lack of interest for others and is unaware of their feelings and the feelings of others. When they do something hurtful to their victim, they show no signs of empathy or desire to help. They lack self-control and react strictly on impulse.

- **Sadism**

This is a trait where the person finds it extremely satisfying to inflict pain on others. To inflict physical harm and emotional abuse on their victim gives a sadist the utmost pleasure and sometimes feel orgasmic to them.

- **Spitefulness**

This means that someone will do anything to retaliate against you even when you know you have done nothing wrong. They will go so far to retaliate or inflict torture to their victim that it may also hurt themselves.

People who consume these behaviors or show these signs are likely to have low self-esteem and cannot accept that other people are more successful than they are. They will show extreme signs of jealousy and do whatever they can in their power, to have what the victim has or to be better than the victim.

How Do People Develop a Dark Personality?

Whether we want to accept this aspect or not, it is a proven fact that all humans have the potential to be evil-minded. Well, this can stem from someone's past, or it can be nurtured into the way someone has grown up, such as previous life experiences they may have had.

As children, we often view the world and make our judgments based on our influences and way of life provided by our parents or guardians. If a child does not feel their superiors unconditionally love them, they will start to develop low self-esteem and lose confidence. Their perception of trust is defined, and they will continue to try harder and harder at gaining the love and attention they so desperately need. An example of this is when a child gets an A, and their superior asks if they can get an A+ next time. This shows the child that their A is not good enough and there is no reward for their behavior. As this continues to happen, the child may only feel worthwhile or loved in their parents' eyes when they are doing their best, and this creates a lifelong pattern of having to chase success while confusing success with happiness.

Another situation is if a child never feels good enough or is continuously compared to their siblings. The parent will pick a "favorite" child and devalue the rest. This household consists of having a parent who is already narcissistic and never thinks their children are good enough because of their self-deprecating values. A child who grows up with a narcissistic parent or superior tends to be more angry, defiant, and humiliated, thus resulting in adult narcissistic behaviors themselves.

Aside from this, there is no real explanation as to why or how someone develops a dark personality. It can be defined as having a rough childhood, being abused, hurt, and continuously let down, if you had a great childhood but got bullied in school, further resulting in hatred toward others and always protecting yourself and your family. Death can sometimes trigger a dark personality. Anything can trigger someone to become more ominous than they are as we all have dark attributes that we try to ignore. Anything can unleash the darker side in our-selves, and eventually, if someone were to get pushed far enough, they can develop their bad traits more dominantly. The fine line between good and bad is that some of us choose to embrace the bad and act upon those impulses whereas others choose not to, giving them more self-control.

Another thing to understand is that once someone gives into the dark side of themselves, they will start to realize that manipulation tactics work and will become addicted to the outcome of their newfound techniques. Once one understands that they can control the world around them to benefit themselves through many shady tactics, this is where the true development of dark personalities come from.

Chapter 2
The Dark Triad

The dark triad is a term relating to the group of three distinct dark personality traits. These personalities include narcissism, Machiavellianism, and psychopathy. People that have high scores in these traits are more inclined to commit crimes, cause social distress, and create extreme problems for a company. People with these traits can use their techniques for selfish success such as being promoted in jobs like law enforcement, clinical psychology, and business management.

Narcissism is characterized by egotism, arrogance, and lack of empathy. Machiavellianism is characterized by manipulation, cynicism, lack of morals, and deception. Psychopathy is characterized by being antisocial, acting on impulse, being selfish, lacking remorse, and having little to no feeling, seeming insensitive to other people's opinions and themselves. The most common trait these personality types share on the "big five personality test" is low agreeableness.

What makes these personalities different from one another is that they each have a certain way about how they prefer to handle things. They each have behavioral and cognitive differences which make them all unique but similar. However, the dark triad traits are found to be genetic but have individual differences in the genes. Machiavellianism seems to be proven less genetic than the other two.

One thing you should understand about the dark-triad traits is that none of these characteristics can be changed in someone if they have it or show signs of having it. This is because it is part of their core personality, and sometimes the offender doesn't even know they are classified as being part of the dark triad group. These types of people can go on living life trying to feel an emotion and trying to be a part of society known as the "norm,". If you find yourself being any of these three, then it's down to you to change, which is going to take a lot of work and soul searching.

How to Identify Each Individual

Machiavellianism

The word comes from an Italian diplomat Niccolo Machiavelli, who wrote the book The Prince, which was interpreted as a certification of the dark arts of deceit. Traits of Machiavellianism include things like deviousness, manipulation tactics, self-seeking qualities, and lack of morality, and emotions. People who have high scores for this trait show high agreeableness and conscientiousness.

Machiavellianism is more popular in men than in women and is the true art of being unfair and cruel to others to get ahead. This stems from their lack of feelings and emotions for other people, causing them to struggle to grasp the aspect of empathy.

To recognize the signs or behavior of Machiavellianism, you must look for these things in someone:

These people will seem so focused on their own goals, ambitions, and interests that you don't seem to matter or faze them when you try to talk about yours. People with this trait will take power over the ones they love while at the same time they can come across as very charming and confident. When it is convenient for them, they will lie and deceive you to get what they want, and if you are the opposite gender, they will do so using flattery. Because of the lack of morality, empathy, and values in their life, they are a very dangerous group of citizens. It is detrimental to your mental health if you come across someone that seems too patient, has a history of casual relationships, doesn't take credit for their actions and find it difficult to interpret or handle their own emotions. They have a thick wall within their personality which causes it extremely hard to get to know them as well.

There is no known cure for this type of personality trait as with most people; for change to happen, you must be willing to accept you have a problem and be susceptible to help. Most people that have Machiavellianism don't even know that they have this trait, and often when they find out that they do, they won't accept it and go through life okay with who they are as they are very egotistical. Only a trained professional therapist that has experience in dark triad counseling can scratch the surface by using cognitive behavioral therapy. Unless it is court ordered or pressured to see a counselor for this trait, the person themselves are most likely not going to go as they also struggle in trusting and becoming close to people.

Narcissism

The word narcissism comes from a Greek hunter named Narcissus. He fell in love with his reflection whilst looking at himself in a pool of water which led him to drowned. Traits of this personality type can include being considerably selfish, conceited, arrogant, having no sense of compassion, and not taking kindly to criticism. People who score high in this trait show high numbers to extraversion and openness while scoring low in agreeableness.

It is important to know that you cannot change someone with this disorderly trait as their narrow-minded behavior will continue to repeat over and over again no matter what you do or don't do for them.

An example here would be, if someone's behavior in a relationship is that they are always demanding attention and trying to get you to admire them excessively. They often ask for too much, and when you cannot for fill their neediness they so desire, they will become hurtful and act superior to you thinking they are better while taking advantage of you in every way. They will express the exaggerated need to be reassured as they can create stories about you in their head so that whatever you do will never be good enough for their standards, thus leaving you wounded and mentally abused.

Another example of this you could be in the workplace, when someone may chat with their coworkers a lot, doing everything in their power to get to know them and impress them with their charm. As they need to feel superior, they gain their coworkers' trust by making promises (which they don't keep) becoming closer to them in a short amount of time. Once they become close, they will take credit for your work, and throw you under the bus without thinking twice about it. As an employer or a leader, they may single their employee they're victimizing out degrading those that are in a higher rank than them while having positive, great things to say to their face—being two-faced.

When dealing with a narcissistic character, a few things to watch out for are their words, emotions, and behaviors:

For words being used by someone who has narcissistic traits, watch out for words and sentences that lack compassion and interest. Once they think they have you and you aren't going anywhere, they will lose interest in you very quickly. If you decide to open up to them and show them your weaknesses, they will rarely take interest and be too quick to turn the conversation around on themselves. However, reversed when you point the blame to them, they will find ways to make you realize you are to blame and not them. If a narcissist gets turned down for a job or rejected by a girl, they will become overly obsessed with proving that they are better going out of their way to make the person who denied them feel bad. This is because of their egotistic nature and how superior they find themselves to be.

For emotions when dealing with someone with this trait, pay attention to how you feel when you're around them. If they seem too good to be true showering you with compliments and if you have a euphoric feeling when around them, this can be a warning sign. People who act in this way are not whom they may seem and will use their charm to get close to you as a way of winning rather than having and keeping. You are a game to them, nothing more as they will lack empathy for others' feelings. Later in a relationship, you may notice that you feel lesser than them as it is so automatic for them to build themselves up while tearing you down in the process. At first, you may not realize it. When a narcissist is in a group of people, they always seem to point the attention on themselves because they lack interest for what anyone else has to say. This is called "sucking up" all the oxygen in the room.

For behavior, pay attention to what they do over what they say. They tend to have distracting and convincing words to make up for their insensitive behavior. They rarely own up to what they have done and repoint the blame on you when you call them out on their behavior. They are very quick with their words finding every reason to defend themselves against you resulting in extreme communication problems. A great way to test their behavior is by asking them to do something like letting you know if they will be late coming home, and if they try to please and satisfy your request, then you may have nothing to worry about. However, if they don't then to end the relationship may be in the best for both of you as you cannot change the way this person behaves or acts.

It is good to remember a narcissistic person will never be blamed or take the blame upon themselves. It will always be yours or someone else's fault even for things they did to themselves. If they didn't get promoted, they would lash out at the closest person to them or their spouse's family as to point the blame on them. Nothing you do is ever going to be good enough as their expectations of you are always going to be just beyond your reach. They will humiliate children in public, sabotaging a coworker, or verbally attacking a friend or colleague. They will become obsessive to damaging relationships by angry venting on social media, creating arguments when there is nothing to fight about, or creating an atmosphere that is toxic for them and everyone around them. At the same time, when their relationship starts to fall apart, they will go back to flattery and charm to fix it as a "winning" technique. This is to keep their victim close, but at the same time not letting them get close enough to them.

Psychopathy

Personality traits associated with psychopathy include lack of feeling for compassion and remorse, antisocial behavior, and using techniques such as manipulation to get to people while being unpredictable in their actions. Take note that there is a difference between having psychopathic traits and being a complete psychopath. Psychopathy has been found to reflect all the "big five" personality factors making up who they are, agreeableness, conscientious, neuroticism, and openness leave the scale between the elements balanced. People who score high on the psychopathy scale show low levels of empathy and high levels of impulsivity and thrill-seeking behaviors.

Psychopathy is hard to spot in an individual because they can seem very ordinary on the outside while lacking compassion and a sense of right and wrong underneath the surface. They put on a charming mask. It works to become vindictive, volatile, and often (but not always) criminally inclined. It is important to note that a psychopath and a sociopath are different. A sociopath refers to a person being antisocial in association with environmental factors. A person with psychopathic traits is raised with violent surroundings causing their characteristics to be born with.

Psychopaths can understand and relate to people as they have no difficulty understanding what they think, want, or believe. Because of this understanding, they can further use their skills of deception and brainwashing to their advantage as they can pinpoint what the other person desires, using it to their advantage. However, this understanding is not automatic for them like most people. It is hard to determine whether someone has psychopathic traits because it seems the offender can switch the characteristics of psychopathy on and off. They can explain in full detail with no remorse or feeling how they managed to hurt, torture, or even kill someone, and at the same time understand how the person questioning them feels about it.

The differences between these three distinct personality types are they each have a different focus while at the same time all have the same goal which is putting themselves first to get whatever they want.

Machiavellianism manipulates others to gain personal skill, power, goals, or achievement. Narcissism believes they deserve all the attention and that they need to be treated differently than others as being unique or better. Psychopathy revolves around being insensitive to how they feel while still understanding the needs and wants of the people around them.

In conclusion to the traits identified by the dark triad, here is a summary on what to look out for in someone you may suspect might be any of the three:

- They manipulate others to extreme measures to get their own way.
- They compulsively lie to get their own way.
- They come off as charming or excessively flirt or compliment you.

- They exploit to get ahead.
- They lack sympathy, remorse, compassion, and empathy for others.
- They have a hard time being interested in morality views.
- They come off as insensitive, brutal, cruel, and spiteful.
- They seem to want affection or attention always and become clingy.
- They seek to be superior against others and often compare themselves.

The Dirty Dozen Test

The dirty dozen test consists of four studies and results in the testing for people with Machiavellianism, narcissism, and psychopathy. This test consists of ninety questions and items spread across three scales. This is called the "dirty dozen" test and determines the likelihood of the dark triad in people.

There are two reasons the dirty dozen test was created to measure the dark triad. First, each calculation has its unique response and limitations. Example, the Mach IV (measure to calculate Machiavellianism) is biased by social desirability. The Mach IV did not exceed .70 on the twenty-item scale, which is considered a low number. The NPI (narcissistic personality inventory) used to measure narcissism is composed of different questions which can be problematic.

Secondly, when studying the dark triad through a series of questions on the dirty dozen test, the screening also uses the "big five" identity test. The "big five" identity test comprises five principle identity characteristics making up an entire extraversion, neuroticism, receptiveness, conscience, and suitability. This test is a general sense of questions asking the student questions like on a scale of one to five would you strongly agree or strongly disagree. However, this test is very long and time-consuming, so the researchers of the dirty dozen testing used other measures and studies that are more efficient and time effective for both the researchers and the participants. There were four studies based around the dirty dozen in figuring out what traits resemble the dark triad.

To determine whether a participant is subjected to being a part of the dark triad, the dirty dozen (consisting of all three traits) will show results that are negative with agreeableness and positive with short-term mating and aggressiveness. Evidence proves that men score higher than women on all three of the dark triad traits. In two studies, researchers develop the calculations from the tests through principal components analyses (known as PCA's) and confirmatory factor analyses (also known as CFA's), also validating the dirty dozen through assessment of the nomological network.

In a third study, they test the consistency of over time process within a matter of 3 weeks as this can define the features of personality traits. Which also results in enough evidence claiming that the test and its usefulness is correct. Finally, in the fourth study, researchers refine their measure by simplifying a double-barreled item, improve the internal consistency of the scale, and again confirm the dark triad dirty dozen's factor structure.

Study 1

Researchers created twenty-two applicant items inspired by the original dark triad measures. Study one consisted of comparing and combining the dark triad traits with that of the "big five" and measures of mating results. The method was 273 psychology students composed of ninety men and 183 women between the ages of eighteen and forty-seven years old. Ten people at a time sat in a lab and completed surveys; once finished, they were thanked and sent off on their way.

By using the big five inventory, researchers were able to accurately assess the big five personality dimensions using a response scale from one to five. Narcissism was assessed with the forty-item NPI. The questions to determine an NPI were "I have a natural talent for influencing people" and "I am not good at influencing people." When the total number was summed up for narcissistic students, their score equaled to .80. Psychopathy was assessed with the thirty-one-item scale 111 (Roman numeral 3). The questions that were asked were, "I enjoy driving at high speeds," and, "I think I could beat a lie detector." The total number for psychopathy students equaled to .74. Machiavellianism was assessed by a twenty-item Mach IV. The questions that followed this screening were, "It's hard to get ahead without cutting corners here and there," and "People suffering from incurable illnesses should have the decision of being killed easily." The outcome to tell if an understudy was a Machiavellian equaled to .65.

When everything was said and done, the researchers totaled all three scales together to give the dark triad result score. To have a result they conducted a separate PCAs and internal consistency analyses for each calculation.

The next three studies followed a similar structure and method to study one and got almost identical results in how to tell if someone had traits consisting of the dark triad.

Chapter 3

THE POWER OF PERSUASION

No matter what we do or where we are in life, we are always being persuaded to do something, whether it's by our colleagues, friends, family, strangers, the media, or the government. It is done very discreetly, but it is happening to us every day. Some people are better at the art of persuasion than others making the world their playground, while others dive deep in emotional disappointment for their efforts.

This chapter will teach you the different techniques on persuasion and what is considered harmful or dark persuasion. What the differences are between the two using solid examples, and understanding how to use persuasion to get your way with others.

The Techniques of Persuasion

There are six different persuasion techniques: reciprocation, social proof, commitment and consistency, liking, authority, and scarcity. These techniques can be used for proper uses and negative uses. The good techniques of persuasion mean if you—the customer—benefits from whatever it is that the persuader—friend or foe—is trying to get you to do, buy, have, or explain something. Good persuasion means to have both parties benefit from whatever it is you or the other person is persuading. Dark persuasion consists of the fact that only one party or person benefits from the situation. The difference between persuasion and dark persuasion is the intent behind the effective tactics. So let's take a look at the six different types of persuasion:

1. Reciprocation

When you are in a mall or shopping around Christmas or holiday seasons, you sometimes may find that a salesperson will reach out and offer you hand cream, perfume, or some other product that will grab your attention. If you are interested and give them attention, they will persuade you to buy some of this or some of that constantly asking for more.

As a natural human instinct, we want to give back to those who give to us. This is a form of cooperation between building relationship and other active types of bonds. When trying to persuade through reciprocation, you want to try to be positive and give useful positive information, resulting in a good experience.

2. Social Proof

A good example of social proof is to watch something funny, and then notice the laughter from the audience behind the scenes of shows (like The Big Bang Theory or Friends). Then try to re-watch the same episode, but this time with the silence of no laughter from the background crowd. You will realize the meant-to-be-funny parts are not all that funny anymore. According to recent facts, we will laugh longer and harder if the background crowds on shows are laughing too. This is called social proof.

If we see that others are doing something positive or negative, we are influenced by social evidence that what we are being persuaded to do is okay. Do you find in public situations something to you seems awkward or funny, but instead of reacting you will take a scan across the room to see if others noticed or feel the way you do? This is to ensure our reaction to the scenario is acceptable or "correct." People skilled in persuasion techniques will use this against customers like us because they know the frame of mind "if everyone else is doing it, or having it, I must too."

3. Commitment and Consistency

As we have grown into society, the media and the world around us make us know that common sense is to keep our word when we commit to something and we should consistently keep that behavior. This is being noble and honest. We don't like being called "wishy-washy" or indecisive, so we strive to commit and be consistent when it comes to this. If we don't then we may face and feel social shame being labeled as inconsistent.

Commitment and consistency persuasion techniques are used on people to "get their foot in the door." An example would be a business person or persuader will request something small of you, and then if you say yes, they will strike again asking for something bigger the next time. This is a way for the persuader to get to know your likes and dislikes so they can expect you to say yes again and again. Before you know it, you are committing to them through consistency and getting asked bigger and bigger requests that you can't say no to.

4. Liking

This technique consists of people that know what you like, based on previous tasks or orders you have done or made. We tend to say yes when we feel important to a company such as Avon or Scentsy. A typical sales technique is to make the customer feel special in such a way that they come back for more and more. Ever notice how when you stop buying things from these companies, they don't seem to notice you exist anymore? But then a few months down the road when you have forgotten about their company or business, you get an email or a phone call reminding you that you are still important to them and that they haven't seen you in a while. Then you are back in the triangle again becoming a valued customer. This is called the liking persuasion technique.

5. Authority

Here's some examples of authority persuasion: A friend may tell us that we might have a health problem, but we choose not to believe them, therefore we get rushed to hospital a few weeks later, and being told by the doctor that we have a health problem, leading us to be quick to believe what the doctor tells us. When we are young we get told that brushing our teeth will keep the dentist away, even though we still grow up forgetting to brush our teeth and after going to the dentist just to be told the same thing. But when we were young, we didn't believe our peers until we got older and trusted the authority. This is known as authority persuasion.

The fact of this is that the authorities have more knowledge in the field that they are in. Doctors and professionals have explicit knowledge in their professions that our friends and family members may not know much about, and therefore we will believe authorities over our close relationships even if they are proven right. It also gives us reassurance to point the blame when we get misinformed.

6. Scarcity

If you have ever watched an infomercial, you know their tactics sound a little like this: "This is a limited time offer. Call or subscribe now to get a discount or promo code." This is a tried and true technique persuader will use to get you to buy their product or request. When there is scarce resource surrounding their topic, this is when the person persuading you is in competition with other marketers because of the scarcity in the resources.

The idea behind this technique is to convince you that you are missing out on something and if you don't act immediately, you could be at a great loss. The persuader knows that people are motivated by the thought of losing something over the thought of gaining something for a better or equal value.

In conclusion to these techniques, it is essential that you understand the tactics used, as these six techniques can be used almost anywhere with just about anything. To understand persuasion, you first must put the facts together. The goal is to build honor, trust, and consistency upon your presence.

The Fine Line between Manipulation and Persuasion

As said before, dark persuasion is based on the use of its intent. Marketers and businesses will use persuasion techniques to help you understand why you must choose them whether their purpose is for good, where it will benefit both parties, or bad, where it will only benefit them. Now the same goes for manipulation. If someone were to use dark persuasion techniques, they are trying to manipulate you in some sort of way. Manipulation means to control or prey upon someone's misfortune to get what they want, which is the same tactics used for dark persuasion.

The real difference is based on three core aspects: the intent behind the desire to persuade someone, how accurate the process is, and the benefit or impact and the individual. Manipulation is to fool, control, or orchestrate the other person into doing something, buying something, or believing something that is false in a persuasive kind of way. This can leave the victim harmed or without benefit before they even know. Another way manipulation works is if the persuader moves their victim to the point of view that only benefits themselves. Now if the persuader doesn't use their persuasion skills correctly, then it leaves their victim less receptive to the idea because they will know that they aren't being benefitted.

Here is an example of manipulative, dark persuasion:

Say for instance i was selling a vehicle, I knew all about manipulation, and I had a plan to persuade my customer. This customer walked into my store and made it known that she had a family with four kids, the request was to look for a family-oriented vehicle. But instead of selling them a family-oriented vehicle, I persuaded my customer to buy a two-seater convertible by telling them that it would bring back their youth. I preceded to say that their kids would love her more because of the nice vehicle she has just bought. It would be teaching her kids to follow their youthful dreams no matter what. Meanwhile, I know that I would be making twice the commission on that car rather than a car that was more suitable for her. She drives off her stylish convertible, thinking she won the better deal, and here I am sitting here grinning from ear to ear, knowing the paycheck I am about to get because of that arrangement.

That's manipulation!

Now looking on the other scale of things, if that same person came to me and said they just wanted a stylish convertible, even knowing they had four kids, but they just wanted to blow some money. I could turn around knowing the same persuasion tactics I used in the first example but instead, I convinced the woman it was a better idea to buy the family-oriented vehicle because it would be in her best interest. I would lay out the facts, and at the end of the day, she drives off happy that she made the right decision about the family car.

This is persuasion not manipulation.

In the first example, I am using dark persuasion to benefit myself without my customer knowing. I will get a better paycheck, leadership skills in my job, and also i'd get bonus points with my boss. The customer, however drives away with the car they love but may have complications down the road with their family, having to buy another car. Because I don't care (having a lack of empathy) getting what I wanted out of the deal (manipulation), I won't see this customer again, and so it doesn't matter (lack of morality). Let's say for instance she comes back to me and gets upset with me for convincing her to buy the vehicle she didn't want, I could just say, I suggested, and you bought it, this is not at all my fault, also taking no responsibility for my actions because this is the way I set things up from the start.

How to Persuade People

Now that we know the definition of persuasion and the difference between the good and bad techniques, we can further investigate how to persuade people ourselves. Whether you use it for good or bad will depend on the reason for why you are persuading to begin with.

There are three steps to persuading someone to do what you want. You must use effective communication skills, listen, and learn what the other wants and needs and then plan your moves. Let's look:

1. **Speak Effectively**
a) **Tell a good story.**

When we want someone to do something for us, we need to share personal or informative information to get them to relate. Start at the beginning and talk about the request at hand. Share how you arrived here by opening their minds to the experiences you have gone through, being careful to understand their feedback. Once they know what your story is, they will be more likely to share theirs. You just got an inside scoop to persuading them into what you want by containing more information about them.

b) **Use ethos (a speaker's credibility), pathos (emotional appeals), and logos (appeals to logic).**

When conversing with the person, you are trying to persuade—or manipulate—include in your story information about your credibility, provide a logical argument, and find their weaknesses to exploit. Tug on their emotional strings. Explaining your credentials will help them trust you, creating and mastering your bond. Once the bond is stable, talk about the logical reasoning behind your request still appealing to their interests. Once this stage is complete, you can further break out their weaknesses and get them emotionally invested by having them relate to your story backed by facts using the trust you have gained from them from the beginning.

c) Prioritize your order of communication.

One mistake a lot of persuaders make is sweet talking first. This will come off as beguiling, and your customer or victim will lose interest quickly. Instead, be straight up and forward with your request and ask for exactly what you want bluntly but respectively. After you have done this, put on the charm. The goal to this is making the customer feel they want to help you, rather than feeling like you must suck up for them to help you.

d) Don't ask them to decide right away.

As human nature, it is relevant that most people do not like to make decisions. When you ask them to make choices, they are more likely to think about it longer and come up with all the pros and cons which stalls time. The point is to ask for what you need and to convince them why it's a good idea to say yes. The last thing you want to do is cause them stress, so it is much easier to get someone to say yes rather than waiting for them to say no.

e) Speak positively and with confidence

People tend to respond to people with confidence and a sense that they know what their influencer is talking about. When you declare positive statements effectively, your customer will be more inclined to listen. Instead of saying, "Don't hesitate to call me," say, "Give me a call on Monday."

2. Listen Effectively

a) Start with small talk.

Make sure they are relaxed or in a comfortable environment. Ask them about their lives and engage with them. Create a casual atmosphere with the person you are trying to persuade by breaking the ice and having a friendly small chat. People are more willing to listen and do when they know you are wanting to become a friend first. When they tell you what they were thinking of doing, that gives you the open door to ask them more about their ideas, continually engaging with them to make them feel special and noticed.

b) Notice their body language.

Match your customer's body language to forge an emotional bond with them. Mirroring someone's body language tells them that you are like them and want and need the same things.

c) Listen more and speak less.

The more someone talks, the more you can understand their hopes, desires, and what they expect. This is crucial for a successful persuasion tactic. People enjoy talking more than listening, so if you give them the freedom to speak, then you can understand and plot more ways on how to persuade them for your benefit. Make sure to respond to their topic and ask questions; this shows them you are listening and can be trusted.

d) "Fill in the blanks."

When you ask someone a direct question, sometimes it may trigger feelings of being put on the spot. So use sentences to convince rather than a conversation filled with questions for them to choose. For example, instead of saying, "Would you like to buy a car?" say, "If you bought a car, I think you would feel..." and allow them to finish the sentence or end it with something positive and original.

e) Sway the conversation toward a more needs focused ideal.

By listening to them and following the previous steps, you should have a better understanding of what they need. Then once you've understood what they need, you can share some of your needs as well so that they can relate to you. When someone can relate to your needs, it will be easier for you to determine how they can help you or how you can help them, whichever way you decide to go.

3. Plan in Motion

a) Choose the right person.

The best person or victim to persuade is the person you are closest to and has the best emotional stability—someone that may need you as well as much as you need them.

b) Wait for the right time.

Choosing the right time like after lunch is usually best. People are more likely to listen and negotiate if they are not hungry. Most people get what's called "hangry"—

this is when you are so hungry that you become irritable or grumpy. Hunger often causes things like anxiety, tension, and negative feelings so choosing the right time to persuade will make it easier to succeed.

c) Help to be helped.

A technique called reciprocity can build trust and close bonds. Set your plan to help the person first; in return, ask them a few days later for their help. As stated in the previous heading, people will be more susceptible to help you if you do something for them.

d) Choose the right situation

When people are persuaded to do something, their environment should be friendly yet business like. A coffee shop, restaurant, or private home will work wonders. The atmosphere is what will help you the most when trying to persuade someone for yours or their benefit.

e) Rehearse your speech.

Don't go into the conversation with someone blindly only to end up winging it. First, practice at home in the mirror keeping in mind it is good to make a good impression. You must come across as knowing what you are talking about. Someone who is focused and has all their facts in place are normally the type of people to listen to. Once you have it dialed down in the mirror, practice with someone you know and see if it works on them.

Chapter 4

Undetectable Mind Control

Undetectable mind control is when someone controls your mind without you noticing or don't even realize. It can also be reversed if you are managing someone else's mind; while they don't even understand or notice, you are using undetected mind control. So what exactly is mind control? Mind control is when someone uses the ability of manipulation through persuasion techniques to take over their victims' sense of power such as the way they think, behave, feel, and decide. A way to enable this is through hypnosis. Undetected mind control is the deadliest kind of mind control there is.

When someone knows or has intuitive that they are mind-controlled, later that gives them a chance to object verbally, physically, and mentally. If the person does not detect that their mind is being monitored, then they won't have enough time to build walls or run from the subject in time. Two types of undetected mind control tactics are interpersonal interactions and the use of media. Because of the use of smartphones and laptops, we have some of the coldest walking manipulators on earth.

How to Tell if You Are Being Mind-Controlled

First, you must understand and learn all there is to know about mind control. If you know the signs, then you can further forego the steps to get away from it if you need. A big part of mind control is involuntary persuasion. As learned in the previous chapter, this is when someone manipulates you to do their bidding which puts you—the victim—under serious stress which can cause anxiety.

The second thing to look out for is a discreet control. A narcissist or personality of the dark triad will use trigger statements to control you. This is when they tell you of how they feel to get you upset or feel empathy for them, so they can remind you of how you are supposed to think, feel, and act.

At the start of this guide we mentioned about the dark triad and the traits that people have. Try and remember these and try to see if you notice any of these signs in your relationship or from a person you know, as you could be at risk of them being able to control your mind. These people have no empathy or emotion, so they will act selfishly and spin your words around to make you understand they aren't controlling you. If you feel isolated from others and think that if you were to leave them or live without them, it would leave you with nothing, then you have already been controlled, and it's a good time to get out while you can, and seek professional help.

These behaviors and techniques from the controller will leave you scared and filled with uncertainty that when you do finally escape, there is none. Or you feel there is no way out. If you try to explain to the authorities, they will look at it like you may be paranoid, and it isn't enough of a case to make, as from the outside it seems like you are in an argument.

However, there are ways you can escape. Reaching out for support through a therapist or a close relationship to you will help, and together you can brainstorm ideas of how to outsmart your victimizer. The process to escape doesn't happen overnight and will take time as there is no quick fix. Understand and accept that because of the way they have controlled you; you will consistently find it hard to trust yourself and others around you. The controller may have a hold on every person involved with your life so try to be discreet. Keep in mind that your self-esteem levels may have dropped, and your trust forms into paranoia, which may affect your decisions as if you feel your being watched all the time. Once you get out though, write what your experience was, how you felt, and what you went through so that the pattern doesn't repeat itself.

So let's rehash more simplistically. Here are five ways you can tell if someone is trying to control you.

Isolation

If the victimizer has you all to themselves with no one to turn to and almost nowhere to run, you're most likely under their control. A simple way they do this is by telling you that the new friend you made has something wrong with them and that you should be cautious. If you love them, then that is exactly what you will do, but some people get to the point of being so overly cautious that they would chase their new friend away, leaving them where they started with just their victimizer. The manipulator will do this to every relationship you have, persuading you to think there is no one you can trust but them because they have your best interest at heart.

Moody Behavior

If your partner seems childish and gets upset when they don't get their way, it can be one of the first sign's control is starting. If you are changing the way you act and think because you don't want to create an argument, then this is a for sure sign they already took your mind over. When you change the way you think, how you feel about certain things, and the way you act around this person or anywhere because of them, you are in the middle of a total controlling relationship. The way you were before you met this person is the way you should be, not having to change for anyone.

Meta-Communication

This is communication in which the victimizer gives you different body language than what they are actually saying. They have a hard time communicating their issue, and so they say nothing, clarifying that there is something wrong by their stand-offish behavior. This is a technique they use against you later. If this happens a lot and you ignore it, they can point the blame to you, saying that you don't care about them and that you should have known something wasn't right. Leaving you feeling you have to walk on "eggshells" later.

Neuro-linguistic Programming

NLP is a tactic manipulators use to layer thoughts using language into a person's unconscious mind without them even knowing about it. An example of this is, if a person is visually orientated, then the victimizer will use pictures and visual clues to plant messages inside the brain. If a person learns better by listening, then the victimizer will use secret auditory signals to get inside the mind without the victim being consciously aware of it.

Uncompromising Rules

Have you ever felt like your spouse set expectations too high or set you up for failure so you argue about it later? This is a form of undetected mind control. Some examples are, meet impossible deadlines like grabbing them a coffee when the store is twenty minutes away in five feet of snow, but they want it in ten minutes. Your life seems so structured that everything you do has to be planned out, and if there is one mistake, it's game over. Or when you don't know what will happen, but they need an explanation, and without reason, you pay serious consequences. What they are doing to you is taking your decisions and making you rethink, and doublethink everything you do so you follow a strict set of behaviors not to upset them. This is so you stop thinking for yourself and they can implant their agenda into your head.

If any of these techniques sound familiar or similar to you, then you should start thinking about ways to combat it or get out. As stated briefly before, people who do this stuff cannot be changed. They will change if they want to, and most times, they don't even know they are doing it because they wire their brains this way. There is no rationalizing with them, and there is no negotiating. You are in a vicious cycle, and it's your choice on what to do next.

How to Use Mind Control on People

So now we have learned how people can use mind control on us, let's flip the tables, and learn about how to use mind control on others. Again, just like the victimizer, learn the way people think, act and behave. Become an expert at analyzing people.

The first thing you need to do is to get to know your victim. Get inside their heads and understand their likes and dislikes. Know their world, who they talk to, what they do, what their schedule and routine is, what their hopes and dreams are, and their fears and failures. To do this, become attractive to them—become whoever your victim needs or wants you to be. This way it will make it easier for them to open up to you. The key to why you need to know the person is because when this person expresses a specific emotion, you can guess what actions he or she will take next. For example, if your boss or supervisor shouts or yells when they get angry but stops doing it when he feels shame or guilt, then making him feel guilty will force him to treat you better and strive to make you happy.

How to Use Emotions to Control People

Fear—when someone acts mighty to you, build up the confidence to act mightier than him, and he or she will shut down and not entertain the idea further.

Guilt—when someone gets angry or acts negatively but is affected by shame, then induce that it upsets you, and the person will back down.

Ego involvement—those that are arrogant and care about the way people look at them, tell them that everyone thinks you will not last, or that your friendship will fall apart if (Then state your Reason). Usually, this person will do everything in their power to make the problems better to preserve their reputation and ego.

Addiction—entice the person that has an addiction problem with whatever their addiction is, and they will bend under your thumb to get what they want, by pleasing you, as you become the source.

Anger—when an angry person yells at you or someone else, stand up to them with your anger. They will usually back down if your anger trumps theirs. It goes against the saying fighting fire with fire, but it can work to control their minds. They may think twice about being angry with you the next time.

By having an understanding of this person, you can see what emotion they have the most, in which you know which one to entice or induce more of. By doing this, it helps you gain control, forcing them to do as you want them to do by persuasion, brainwashing, or manipulation techniques.

How to Analyze Someone

To analyze means to study or examine something precisely and carefully methodologically. So when we analyze people, it is safe to say we are psychoanalyzing the individual. Psychiatrists and psychologists and professionals of the doctorate field will use this technique to understand further the way their mind works to create a successful treatment. To psychoanalyze someone, you must first let go of all preconceptions and judgment. You need to open your mind to understand the person in front of you fully. People who excel in reading, who are trained to see the invisible, and can read between the lines. There are three techniques to understanding how to read people.

First Technique: Observe Body Language Cues

It is a proven fact that words only make up 7 percent of how we communicate whereas body language and tone of voice make up the rest. Keep in mind not to try so hard to read body language, just sit back and silently observe.

Pay Attention to Appearance

Notice what they may be wearing. If they are buttoned up with shiny shoes, this indicates they may be ambitious people striving for success. If they choose a more casual look like jeans and a t-shirt, this may suggest a laid-back more casual personality. If they wear a tight top with quite a bit of cleavage, they may be the seductive type. Finally, if they are wearing a cross or Buddha pendant, this could indicate spiritual values.

Notice Their Posture

If they hold their head high, this could indicate they are confident. If they walk with their head down or slouch, this could mean they have low self-esteem. Maybe you might notice they arrogantly sway when they walk with a puffed chest. This could be a sign of someone who may have a big ego.

Watch for Physical Movements

When people lean toward something, it means they like that something, when they lean away, it means the opposite. If they cross their legs or arms, it can mean anger, defensiveness, or self-protection. Are they hiding their hands? This can say that they have a secret or could be hiding something. Lip biting and finger fidgeting mean they are uncomfortable and nervous, so it is a way to soothe themselves.

Look at Their Facial Expressions

You can tell a lot about a person's emotions through their facial expressions. A deep frown line indicates excessive worrier or an over-thinker. Crow's feet are joy smile lines. Pursed lips suggest anger, contempt, or bitterness. A clenched jaw signaled tension and built-up frustration.

Second Technique: Listen to Your Gut Instinct

Intuition is what your gut says, not your mind. It stems beyond logic and comes in the form of nonverbal feelings you perceive such as images and gut feelings. When reading someone, what counts the most is who the person is and feeling their aura rather than what they show you. Intuition helps you with this process

Honor Your Intuitive Instinct

In the first meeting, your gut will tell you how to perceive this person based on the first impression. This is an emotive reaction that occurs before you have the time to think. Are you at ease meeting this person or no? This is the trust meter that instinctually tells your brain what your take on this person is or should be.

Feel the Goose Bumps

Goosebumps are intuitive tingles that can either tell us that this person moves us or if they strike a nerve. They can also appear when you experience déjà vu a familiar feeling that you have known or been in this type of presence before, even if you have never met.

Pay Attention to Flashes of Insight

Be aware of the "aha" moments when conversing with someone. If you don't pay attention and take a mental note of this moment, you may miss it because of the rapid thoughts that go through your brain daily.

Notice Intuitive Empathy

When we relate to someone or connect with someone by a more profound meaning beyond explanation, we feel their physical symptoms and emotions. So when you are around someone you are trying to read, notice if you have pains that weren't there or feelings that came out of nowhere and only exist in their presence. This is also classified as sympathy pain.

Third Technique: Sense of Emotional Energy

There is a certain "vibe" each will give off. Similar to intuition, we can sense this vibe based on the emotional energy they portray. Some people give off a feel-good vibe of positive energy, while others may feel like you are suffocating in their presence. This discreet energy can be felt inches to feet away from you.

Sense People's Presence

This is the atmosphere that surrounds us, giving off the overall energy we emit caused by what makes us who we are—dark or light people, happy or sad. When reading people, notice if their presence seems friendly or attractive or if you feel chills up or down your spine making you want to run.

Pay Attention to People's Eyes

When we look into people's eyes, we can learn their energy. The body and the eyes have the same invisible signal telling us who this person portrays themselves as, or who they are. Someone's eyes can say a lot about them such as if they are caring, sexy, tranquil, mean, or angry. If their eyes are hard to read, this may be an indication that they are guarded.

Notice the Feel of Someone Shaking Your Hand or Giving You a Hug

When reaching out to shake someone's hand, notice if you feel warmth, comfortable or confident. Also, see if you want to pull your hand away as quickly as they touched you. What is the texture of their hand? Clammy, signaling nervousness and anxiety, or limp indicating being withdrawn or timid.

Listen to the Tone of Their Voice

While you listen to the person you are conversing with, notice how it makes you feel. Is their tone soft and soothing like your mother or elder, or is it short, snippy, or whiny? Based on these aspects of the sound in their voice, we can tell a lot about someone's emotions.

Chapter 5

Covert Emotional Manipulation

There are many types of manipulation, but the two we are going to discuss in this chapter are covert and psychological. Covert manipulation is when a person uses deceptive and dishonest tactics to change your way of thinking, behavior, and perceptions to gain power over you. Emotional manipulation consists of manipulating you when you are consciously aware, but not aware that the person is managing you. These two are the same. Someone who is skilled in manipulation skills will make sure your self-worth and mental well-being are in their hands.

Techniques of Manipulation

When a victimizer victimizes, their end goal is reflected by one thing, which is gaining power to benefit themselves. The manipulator will exploit in wicked ways, leaving the victim feeling mentally and emotionally exhausted. Some tactics go unnoticed for quite some time, and the damage is hard to fix when it has been done. Update yourself with the tactics so that you will be able to understand and pinpoint when it is happening. Here is a list of tricks manipulators use. It is important to remember this list may not mean that the victimizer is deliberately trying to manipulate you. They may not even know themselves that they are using these tricks.

1. Home court advantage

A manipulative individual may ask you to meet them in a private space such as an office, a home, a car, or other closed spaces. This is so they can exercise dominance and control.

2. Let you communicate first

A cop, salesperson, psychologist, judge, lawyer, and almost everyone in the work field will use the skill of getting you to talk first. This is so they can get inside your head and figure out your weaknesses, your hopes and dreams, ambitions, and fears. Once they know this information, it will be easier for them to exploit you and persuade you for their selfish purposes. They succeed at this by listening, observing, then asking you personal questions.

3. Manipulation of facts

They show very prominent characteristics. They will lie or make excuses for their behavior. They will make you feel guilty for their actions. They are often very good with their words withholding information on a need-to-know basis. Exaggeration and being one-sided is another indication of their manipulation traits.

4. Overwhelm you with statistics

When someone knows more of something than you do, they may make that well-known by throwing their intellect in your face. This is called "intellectual bullying," and they may only do this to feel smarter or better than you. In most cases, they will constantly overwhelm your mind with all the things you didn't know that they know. They will do this in front of people as to get a rise out of how you act. If you don't act, they have succeeded because this means their manipulation has gone unnoticed.

5. Overwhelm you with procedures and methods

Jobs, including law and political enforcement, use documents like paperwork, procedures, laws, and by-laws, committees, and others. This is to stall the victim and make them think their way is the way to think because they are correct. This type of behavior can stop a person from finding the truth, hide flaws, and avoid further examination. The government uses this to maintain power and control while keeping their position.

6. They may raise their voice

As a form of aggressive manipulation, some individuals may raise their voice. They believe that if they raise their voice and display negative emotions, you will become submissive to their compulsion and give them what they desire. Alongside the loud voice, they will use hostile body language such as towering over you and puffing their chest out.

7. Negative surprises

Negative surprises are surprises that put you off balance which lets them gain an emotional advantage. This can consist of low balling you in a negotiation situation, to a sudden task that the victim won't be able to complete or deliver. Usually, this comes without warning and may also result in requests as a means to continue victimizing you.

8. Give you little to no time to make decisions

This is a situation where the victimizer puts you under pressure by applying tension to control you. By doing this, it makes them hopeful that you will crack under pressure and give in to their demands.

9. Negative humor

Negative humor is when someone pokes fun at your weaknesses, making it seem like a joke so it doesn't become that big of a deal. In reaction to this, you may become angry and less secure. An example of this is, making fun of your appearance or intellect, what you have or don't have, making comparisons or bringing up your past and patterns. They do this because it will create a sense of emotional high standard control over you, leaving you humiliated.

10. Constantly judge you

Instead of humor, this is where the perpetrator bluntly makes fun of you and calls your weaknesses out; this is a form of bullying. They strive to make you believe you are not good enough and something must be wrong with you by picking out all your faults and exploiting them. No matter how hard you try, it never seems to be good enough because their expectations are too high leaving absolutely no room for failure. The offender creates a negative focus on you and your flaws without providing a solution to fix or offering any real means of help.

11. The silent treatment

The silent treatment is a good way for them to possess control over your mind, making you question and become uncertain. They do this on purpose to gain mastery manipulation as a type of head game. As you wait and become doubtful, they are on the other end, smiling at themselves, being proud that they have you squirming in your seat.

12. Pretend ignorance

Pretend ignorance is a "passive/aggressive" way to play dumb so that you will take on their responsibilities. This is a way for them to get you to do their "dirty work" so they don't have to. You will find this behavior in children who manipulate their parents into getting them to do their chores or something they don't want to do as procrastination. Some adults will do this as well if they have something to hide or responsibility they are avoiding.

13. Guilt-baiting

Guilt-baiting is a means of targeting the recipient's emotional weaknesses and opening their vulnerability to force them to do as they say or want. Guilt-baiting consists of irrational blame, pulling on heartstrings, and holding someone else responsible for their failure.

14. Victimhood

Victimhood is to play the "victim card" used to exploit the goodness and take advantage of good qualities in someone. They will pull from the recipient's guilty conscience, a sense of responsibility, and protective nature to get them to obtain selfish benefits. Some examples include exaggerated or made-up personal issues, health issues. Dependency and codependency. The manipulator plays weak and powerless to gain sympathy.

Characteristics of a Manipulator

The only reason a manipulator would be interested in you is if they can use you for their own personal gain. They will take what you say and do and twist it around so that you are left confused and unable to recognize yourself. Distorting the truth and lying are the two most significant factors that they will excel at.

The following are five characteristics of a manipulator. This list is provided so that you know and understand what to look for in someone, helping you stay alert and hopefully prevent you from getting pulled into their trap.

1. Selfish

Either they lack insight on how to engage with others or they honestly believe that their way is the only way. When their needs are being met, that is all they care about. Every situation that revolves their world is about them, not caring what others think, feel, and want.

2. No sense of personal space

When it comes to boundaries, offenders do not have them, nor do they respect others. If they get what they want, they don't think about who it hurts. They will crowd your space physically, emotionally, mentally and spiritually and be un-interested of how it affects you. It's like a parasite; they will feed off someone to leave that person to feel exhausted, weakened, and humiliated.

3. A good people reader

A perpetrator will look at their victim and be able to know if they have a good chance at trapping them. They prey on people's sensibilities and conscientiousness. If you are a kind, caring, gentle person, you are at risk of becoming manipulated. A manipulator will spot these good traits in you, and use your personality against you. They become what you need of them first, then they put on the charm until they have you. Then over time leave you broke and confused because they are getting or have gotten what they want from you.

4. Good conversationalists

The way the offender talks about others is more than likely how they are talking about you. They have mastered "triangulation" being where they create scenarios and dynamics that set up for hatred and jealousy while encouraging alienation.

5. They are not who they pretend to be

If a person tried to be good, they would be good. If a person decides to be evil, they will develop negative traits. Usually, what you see is what you get. So if someone were to be deceiving and untrustworthy, that means that is who they are portraying to be. If someone were to be kind and giving that is who they choose to be. If your offender seems too good to be true, it's because they usually are, so listening to your instincts is wise when you get this feeling.

How to Outsmart a Manipulator

We have gone over how to spot a manipulator and what their characteristics and techniques might be, but how do we outsmart them? If you are up against a manipulator, then there is something you may want to keep in mind when dealing with one. Here are some tricks to try.

1. The first thing to do is to avoid the offender. The first sign of techniques or tactics being used on you, divert their energy and run. If you have to make excuses why you can't hang out, do that. If you need to say you are busy, then stick to it. The first and most efficient way to deal with them is to avoid them.

2. Learn to say no. Once you understand the meaning of no and take a stand for yourself so that you don't get pushed around, you will find that life is much easier to live. If saying no makes you feel guilty and you find this causes you to be afraid to say no to people, then this

will only set yourself up to be taken for granted. Which is what a manipulator wants and looks for.

3. Ignore the offender. Ghost them. Walk away from them. Do whatever you need to do if you can't avoid them. This is just another form of avoidance, but if you can't walk away, run away, or say no, then ignoring them is your best bet. If you are around one and cannot get away, then nodding, pretending to listen with an "mhm" now and then is best.

4. Set boundaries. This may be the most important one of them all. At the beginning of any relationship you make, make sure you are very clear about what you will accept and what you want. Make it clear that you will and won't do or tolerate certain things. Whenever you say no or set boundaries, make sure you also add why this is acceptable or unacceptable, that way no misunderstanding takes place. It also shows

confidence that you are a healthy individual who knows what they want and doesn't want.

5. Set goals. When you know what you want, who you want to be, and how you want to get there, it makes it harder for a manipulator to come in and take it from you. You don't have to know the answers right now but setting goals toward your future and for yourself shows that you at least want to try.

6. Get to know someone before you get emotionally invested with that someone. Once you can know for sure that they aren't out to get you, then you can remember to put your trust in them and build a life or friendship based on truth and facts. This isn't easy, and it takes some time to get to know someone—give or take six months to a year.

7. Become someone that they wouldn't want to mess with. At first, put up your walls and create this persona that what you say and do match up. You need to make your personality

prominent in the first couple minutes of meeting someone. Making your first impression a bold one will show a manipulator that you are not the right person to target.

8. Make others aware of this person and your suspicions. Do it discreetly so that you don't get burned in the end, but definitely strive to help others avoid this person. Make sure you have your facts right though, because if you are wrong, then you can really hurt someone's ego and life. You wouldn't want to make a false accusation then destroy their resources so they are left with nothing. The goal is to take their power away, not their life.

Chapter 6
BRAINWASHING

Brainwashing—which is otherwise known by many as mind control, menticide, coercive influence, thought control, thought change and reinstruction—is the idea that suggests that the personality of a human can be either adjusted or constrained by a bunch of mental strategies. Brainwashing is known to work toward reducing your ability to think on your own, to introduce new thoughts and ideas into your mind with the aim of changing your frame of mind, qualities, and beliefs. In brain science, the study of brainwashing, known as thought change, falls into the circle of social impact. Social impact is known as the way people can change the way in which they view life, their convictions, and practices.

For example, there is a technique that works to change a person's behavior who isn't worried about their frame of mind or morals. The training technique, which is also known as the "purposeful publicity strategy," occurs when you don't care about what's being taught and try to change a person's mindset, along with the lines of "Do it since you know it's the correct activity." Brainwashing has a serious type of social impact that combines different ways to deal with changes in somebody's state of mind without the individual's consent. Since brainwashing is such an intrusive practice, it requires the total loyalty of the subject, which is the reason you hear about the brainwash practices happening in jail camps or total factions.

How Brainwashing Works

The brainwasher must have unlimited authority over the objective or person being brainwashed with the goal of controlling the sleep routine, eating, using the washroom and the satisfaction of all other essential human needs rely upon the specialist. In the mentally conditioning procedure, the operator efficiently separates the subject's personality to the point that it doesn't work any longer. The brainwasher replaces it with another list of activities, morals, and ideas that work in the objective's present condition.

While most clinicians trust that mentally programming an individual is conceivable under the correct conditions, some consider it to be far-fetched or possibly as a less extreme type of impact than the media depicts it to be. A few meanings of brainwashing require the danger of physical damage, and under these definitions, most groups don't brainwash since they usually don't physically abuse people. Different definitions depend on "nonphysical compulsion and control" as similar methods for brainwashing. Notwithstanding which definition you use, numerous specialists trust that even under perfect conditions, the injured individual's old personality isn't killed by the procedure. However, it is secluded from everything, and once the "new character" quits being strong, the individual's old temperaments and beliefs will return.

Brainwashing steps and methods for

In the past, it has been established that a multistep procedure that has been developed, which starts with assaults on the detainee's feeling of self and ends with what seems, by all accounts, to be a change in the mindset of the person. Scientists eventually characterized a lot of steps associated with mental conditioning and brainwashing, such as:

- Strike on character
- Blame
- Self-treachery
- Limit
- Tolerance
- Impulse to admit
- Diverting of blame
- Discharging of blame
- Advancement and amicability
- Admission and resurrection

Each of these stages happens in a domain of segregation, which means all "ordinary" social reference focuses are inaccessible, and methods like lack of sleep and ailing health are regularly part of the procedure. There is the risk of physical harm, which adds to the brainwashing.

- Separation of Personality

This involves an attack on the personality of the subject, which includes ideas like, "You are not who you think you are," a deliberate assault on the character or inner self of the subject and his entire mindset. The operator denies everything that makes the identity of the subject, with statements like, "You are not a warrior," "You are not a man," and, "You are not guarding opportunity." The objective is under consistent assault for quite a long time, weeks or months, to the point that he ends up weak, confused and a shadow of himself. Thus his convictions appear to be less strong.

- Blame

You are awful. While the character emergency is setting in, the operator makes a feeling of blame in the objective. He savagely assaults the subject for any "wrongdoing." He may pick on you for everything from the "poorness" of your mindset to the manner in which you eat. You then start to feel a general feeling of insecurity.

- Self-selling out

When the subject is drowning in pitiful blame, the specialist drives him either with the danger of physical damage or of continuation of the psychological assault to hate his family and friends. This selling out of his morals and belief of individuals he feels a feeling of dedication to expanding the disgrace and loss of personality.

- Limit

Who am I, where am I, and what am I expected to do? With his character in an emergency, going through so much disgrace and having sold out what he has dependably had confidence in, the objective may experience what in layman terms is called a "mental meltdown." In brain research, "mental meltdown" is only a gathering of events that can show any number of mental changes. It might include wild crying, great sadness, and general confusion. The objective may have lost his grasp on the real world and have the feeling of being lost and alone. At the point when the objective achieves his limit, his feeling of self is ruined—he has no control over the identity or what's going on. Now, the operator sets up the compulsion to change over to another mindset that will spare the objective from his sadness.

- Leniency

Focusing on a condition of emergency, the brainwasher offers some kindness or relief from the mental torture. He may offer the objective a beverage of water, or pause for a minute to ask the objective what he misses about home. In a condition of breakdown coming about because of repeated mental assault, the objective may encounter a positive feeling and appreciation different from what he's used to, as though the operator has spared his life.

- An impulse to admission

For the first stage of brainwashing, the objective is confronted with the difference between the blame and torment of the personality strike and the sudden show of mercy. The objective may feel a longing to respond to the affection offered to him, and the brainwasher may introduce the idea of admitting fault as a way to removing blame and agony.

Diverting of blame

After long periods of mental breakdown, the objective's blame has lost all significance—he doesn't know what he has done wrong, he realizes he is not right. This makes something of a clean slate that gives the operator a chance to fill in the spaces: He can coerce that feeling of "misleading quality," to anything he desires. The specialist joins the objective's blame to the mindset the operator is attempting to create. The subject comes to trust that it is his mindset that is the reason for his sadness. The complexity among the old and new mentality has been built up: The old mindset is related with mental and physical misery, and the new mindset is related with the likelihood of getting away from the sad mentality.

- Discharging of blame

The troubled target is made to realize that there is a reason for his "bad mindset," that it isn't he himself—this suggests that he can get away from his situation by making a change to the wrong mindset. He is faced with the idea that should simply get rid of the general concepts and behaviors that are related to that particular mindset, and he won't be in pains any longer. The objective can get rid of the sad feeling by admitting to acts related to his old mindset and behavior. With his full acceptance, the objective has finished mentally dismissing his old mindset and actions. It is then up to the specialist to offer a new mindset and behavior to the target.

Conclusion

A procedure of brainwashing like we have just discussed, has not been tried in a research center setting, since it's harming to the objective and would be a wrong exercise. Scientists made these conclusions from direct records of the strategies used by people who brainwashed in the past and different examples of "mental programming" around a similar time. Since different scientists have distinguished mental breakdown from what seems, to be a group of steps that result in a new mindset, which is the reason a few people end up being brainwashed and others don't.

How You Can be Brainwashed

If you have ever watched the film "The Manchurian Candidate," you will see that a successful senator was captured by Korean soldiers and then brainwashed into becoming a sleeper agent for them. The intent behind the brainwashing techniques the Koreans used, was to assassinate the presidential candidate. The film clearly shows that even a successful man can be brainwashed, but in reality, the opposite is more likely to happen.

People that are vulnerable or have low self-esteem are the ones that are more at risk to be brainwashed. These types of people have lost a loved one to death or divorce, been terminated from their job, been forced to homelessness, or have a disorder or an illness that they struggle to accept.

A person who wants to brainwash you, will generally look for your strengths and weaknesses, figure out who you trust and who listens to you. This information is needed to manipulate your beliefs. The brainwashing process starts and takes five steps to do so:

1. **Isolation**

People who have friends and family are dangerous to the predator because friends and family can question their motives, therefore helping the victim to think.

Isolation starts where the offender gets you to love them or create some sort of close bond with them so that you trust them. Once the trust and the relationship are made, over time they start making you question the influences around you. Once this process is complete, the perpetrator will then work on your influences getting them to turn against you after knowing your secrets. Alas, you are isolated without even knowing it. This can take up to a couple of months

2. Self-esteem attacks

When you are in a vulnerable state and feel like no one else cares, the subject hurting you will make a move towards your esteem. If you already have low self-esteem, it becomes easier for them to attack you. The ways they do this is to cause you stress so that you are not able to sleep, then enforce violence and abuse, intimidation, and embarrassment. Eventually, your life will be so controlled, you won't know when a good time is to sleep, eat or even use the washroom.

3. You vs. Them

A brainwasher will break you down so that they can address a better situation than the one you are currently in. By nature, humans are tribal and want to be part of a group. We are social creatures. When the brainwasher puts us in a dynamic group where we can relate to others that are brainwashed, the offender gains more control of you and your environment making you believe it is better where you are then where you were.

4. Blindly listening to them

The end result for a brainwasher is to have you look to them without thinking. Without you noticing, they want you to understand and relate to what they tell you or convince you to do. To achieve this goal, they will generally reward you with positive feedback or things when you listen. However, they will also reverse the effect and use negative punishment for when you don't listen to them.

Another way they can get to you is to chant or say the same thing over and over again. Repetitive phrases are a way to calm the brain, and it is proven that the analytical and repetitive parts of the brain are interchangeable.

5. Testing

A perpetrator will test their subject by committing a criminal act of some kind to see what their victim does or will do. If their victim seems fine and is programmed the way they left them, their test is working. When their analysis is shown positive, it tells them that the subject is still brainwashed, and lets the offender know they still have all control. There is a possibility, however, that the victim can regain their consciousness back and start thinking for themselves, hence, why the tests are in place.

To stop yourself from being brainwashed, you must live by a few rules.

- Don't believe into what you read.

- Don't let scare tactics phase you
- Pay attention to subliminal messages
- Be a leader and think for yourself
- Do not put yourself in a compromisable situation.
- Do your research
- Be unique
- Don't let yourself be isolated.

Help your friends and let other people be aware. If they are being brainwashed, get them out and support them through the withdrawals of the perpetrator.

Dark Psychology and Brainwashing

Dark psychology strategies are used by individuals around us consistently to control, pressure, and impact us to get what they need. Dark psychology is essentially the art and craft of the study of brainwashing and mind control. While Psychology on its own is the study of human conduct and has proven to be vital to our lifestyles, mindsets, activities, and behavior, the term dark psychology is the marvel by which individuals use strategies of inspiration, influence, control, and intimidation to get what they need. As indicated by most specialists, the study related to the term brainwashing occurs in different stages. The idea of mental breakdown and brainwashing involves different robust methods and types of psychological and physical pressure. The subject is quite often in a withdrawn area or a learning area which is usually far from friends and family, where they are around other subjects. The lack of sleep is very typical, as the change in eating regimen and example of dress code and behavioral patterns. Open self-blame is commonly supported under self-investigation. The subject's time is cautiously controlled and loaded up with a vast number of exercises. This backing can appear as addresses, readings, and other gathering exercises. This stage can be as short as a couple of days and can sometimes stretch out for a considerable length of time. It is intended to inspire such feelings as dread, blame, fatigue, and confusion concerning the enlisted.

This initial stage dives deeply into the second phase of mental breakdown in which the subject is urged to "experiment with" different exercises. These exercises may include such things as self-investigation, addresses, asking, and working at gathering related tasks. Such components might instill this act of cooperation as social weight, good manners, authentic interest, or a longing to gain support with power figures. This coordinated effort drives the subject to start to consider the intelligence of the mindset being referred to truly, this gives room to the third phase of brainwashing in which the real change in mindset begins. In this third stage, the subject usually affects the mindset, along these lines creating an especially powerful dependency on friendship. Furthermore, the information given to the subjects is cautiously screened to support the gathering lessons. The subject remains physically and emotionally weak, and this makes it troublesome for the subject to make any personal complaints about the whole process.

In the last phase of influence, starting mindset concerning the gathering and its idea is strengthened to the point that the newcomer comes to acknowledge the lessons and choices that have been instilled while seeing any other purpose that points to the opposite as being very wrong. By this point, the subject has been coaxed into taking a series of open as well as irreversible activities in support of the brainwashing. These exercises involve stress, mental breakdown, and a change in the mindset after some time. As an example, when the Symbionese Liberation Army was influencing Patricia Hearst, she at first was asked to prepare with the gathering. At that point, she was requested to copy a prewritten radio discourse. Next, she was asked to both compose and record such a discussion. She was required to go with the gathering on a bank burglary with an emptied weapon. The level of the behavior that was expected from her kept increasing over time with the gathering.

In this last stage, subjects stay surrounded by the people who carry out the teaching and brainwashing. These people verify the subject's impression of the rules and exercises. Also, they examine and record the subjects change in mindset and total identity change. As per late news reports, these techniques compare near those followed in the preparation of people involved in suicide bombings on planes once they express an underlying readiness to make such a change in their identity. Such people are guarded and confined in houses, lose access to family members, and frequently recordings are made to be used in future publicity endeavors. Specialists take note of that the strategies or stages that are portrayed in the past subheadings arrange a list of strong brainwashing systems and methods. Friend weight is known to be especially powerful when an individual faces a problem.

Individuals' capacity to oppose an idea is especially weakened when they do not have the chance to contemplate the idea because of dread, lack of sleep, and additional overactivity. When like-minded people such as those found in some gatherings talk about a point they happen to agree upon, the outcome is a common mentality, with gathering individuals taking a common conclusion after talking. Essentially, outrageous mentalities also occur when people find out that others share and appreciate their ideas. When people agree to severe and open punishment, they need to support such activities by using any mindset that helps these convictions, a procedure referred to as the "decrease of subjective disharmony." The aims of numerous fanatic gatherings dwell on the human need to feel essential, critical, and part of a social circle, whether it's a religious, political, logical, or notable group. In this passionate setting, the extreme influence related to the term brainwashing is a group of methods that, can inspire amazing changes in both the mindset and behavior of the subjects.

Chapter 7

NEURO-LINGUISTIC PROGRAMMING: THE BASICS

Neuro-linguistic programming is a lot of different aptitudes that communicates with the inner-self. It is a type of communication that consists without speech. To break it up, so it is easier to understand, let's take a look at the individual aspects of the word.

Neuro. This term refers to the mind and brain. It controls the state of mind that affects communication and behavior.

Linguistic. This term refers to the way our mind and body reacts to our language and nonverbal communication. Speech and verbal communication are tools we use to gain insights into the way our brain works, whereas neuro-linguistic programming language teaches us how to access unconscious information.

Programming. This term relates to the volume of the brain that controls the way we change our mind and body state. Programming refers to what you do subconsciously such as your habitual patterns and thoughts, feelings, reactions, beliefs, and traditions. Someone trained in NLP can access this part of the brain by accessing it through conversation so that outdated programmed behaviors can be changed.

So in short, neuro refers to neurology, linguistic relates to language, and programming refers to how both neuro and linguistic come together to make language functions work.

How Does NLP Work

The human language revolving around words makes up only 7 percent of meaningful communication. When someone says something, and then their body language and facial expressions say the opposite, that makes up

93 percent of the communication we use nonverbally. Someone's mindset, attitude, and feelings is an active form of communication. In the world of communication, a whole different way of interacting consists in your mind and through our body language.

Techniques Surrounding NLP

The techniques that follow are powerful and effective when changing how someone experiences and thinks about the world. NLP can transform someone's life since our thoughts and feelings shape our reality. These are the four most impactful techniques that are used:

1. **Dissociation**

Feelings of shyness, nervousness, and sadness, in some situations are automatic or unstoppable. Whether you want to build up the nerves to talk to that person you have a crush on, or if you have to get in front of a crowd and speak publicly. These situations bring on automatic, uncontrollable feelings inside us.

Dissociation can help immensely with these automatic feelings.

a) Identify the emotion that you want to get rid of.
b) Imagine you are of an out-of-body experience, and you can look at yourself. Watch yourself from an observer's perspective.
c) Once this is complete, notice how you feel at that moment. It will change dramatically.
d) If you would like to go one step further, take yourself out of the body that is observing yourself, so you are looking at yourself watch your other self.

2. Content reframing

Reframing means to take a negative situation and make you feel superior by changing the meaning of the situation into something positive. A good example is this: You just ended a bad relationship. You are most likely feeling awful and sad which will be an automatic feeling an in human nature to feel. But by reframing the meaning behind the ending of the relationship, we can ask ourselves "what are the benefits of being single?" Say that you have learned valuable lessons from the previous link and now more doors have opened up to you. Like being free to do what you want, when you want, and you don't have to answer to anyone or have obligations to anyone but yourself. In short, reframing your mind to see a situation differently will give you a positive outlook on your experiences.

3. Anchoring

Anchoring is when you are conditioned to a particular response. Ivan Pavlov experimented with dogs to get this response. He would ring a bell repeatedly while dogs ate, after doing this a bunch of times, the sound made the dogs salivate. Once this happened, even if there were no food, whenever Ivan rang the bell, the dogs would salivate. This is an example of anchoring by creating a conditioned response.

You can accomplish this with yourself if you create emotion with a sound or gesture. As long as you can associate one thing (behavior) with another (thought), then you are anchoring yourself. Do this repeatedly, and every time you do that one thing you associate bad, you can do the other thing that makes your brain positive about it.

4. Getting other people to like you—rapport

This technique consists of silently and discreetly mirroring someone else's body language, tone of voice, and words. We like and get along with people we can relate to. If we imitate other people's actions, our brain sends pleasure sensors which make people feel a sense of liking to anyone who reflects them.

Chapter 8
The Fine Art of Deception

Deception is the act of wrongly advising somebody about the truth of something. Imagine setting off to the doctor for a drug to help with a health concern, and for a while, you take your endorsed medicine to find later that you've been given a fake drug or sugar pill and were not treated for the sickness. Odds are, you will feel furious and baffled because of this trickiness. You may even think that your doctor acted wrongly.

In psychology, deception is far from being a true moral issue. A few doctors and specialists believe that misdirecting somebody who is part of an examination is deceptive and can make people feel clueless concerning the real idea of the test. Others trust that deception is essential since it keeps members from carrying on unnaturally; it is vital that members act in their true manner when they are not being watched or examined.

Indeed, even the most truthful people practice deception, with different examinations demonstrating that the average individual lies a few times each day. A portion of those untruths are huge, yet more frequently, they are seen to be harmless, comments like "That dress looks fine" are sent to maintain a distance from awkward circumstances.

While misleading oneself is commonly seen as hurtful, a few specialists maintain that there are specific sorts of self-deceit—like trusting that you can achieve an aim objective regardless of what might be expected—that can positively affect success.

Analysts have since, hunted down approaches to completely recognize when somebody is lying. A standout amongst the most notable, the polygraph test, has been questionable, and there is some proof that maintains people who suffer from specific mental issues like antisocial personality disorder can't be estimated by polygraphs or other frequently used lie recognition techniques.

Why We Lie

Nobody likes being fooled, and when open figures are caught in a lie, it can turn into an outrage. In any case, while a lot of people pride themselves on their trustworthiness—and try their best to avoid liars, we all need to come to terms with the fact that everybody lies, for a lot of reasons. A few specialists propose that a specific amount of deception might be vital for keeping up a sound working society.

How to Spot a Liar

Being able to spot a liar is a trick that many people feel they have. Few people can boast this ability. Take an example as, if you're talking to somebody you just met, who says that he knows one of your friends, however, this doesn't exactly seem to be accurate for you. It is possible that this person needs something out of you, to get the information that could be used against you. You're naturally hesitant to say anything, but deep down, you know it's possible for this person to know your buddy truly, and here comes your dilemma.

A lot of people are just not great at spotting deception. People usually watch out for signs that will help to spot a liar. However, liars show little or no symptoms that would imply they are telling lies. It's possible that sometimes, people may not be right in their suspicions about liars, but rather, the signs that are supposed to show when somebody is lying are just not reliable. There is also an idea that outward looks may give more signals than the liar's words or actions.

The key to spotting distinguishing deception is entangled by the way that making a decision about apparent versus presented signs isn't equivalent to deciding if an individual's facial expressions is that of someone that is lying or not.

Negative statements turn out to be a test since liars are not great at deliberately appearing to be angry. Specialists call attention to the fact that liars are less productive in faking negative feelings.

Notwithstanding these troubles, specialists trust that people could turn out to be right while recognizing the statement of liars whenever given the correct directions. A survey looked into two methods with regards to deception. In the first of two investigations, undergrad members saw recordings of individuals who were lying or coming clean, viewing these with no sound. The records were made by asking the performing artists to either lie or come clean about the manner in which they were feeling in the wake of having watched a film section of either The Jungle Book (positive emotions) or Sophie's Choice (negative feelings). The members viewing the recordings at that point gave their opinions on who they thought was lying or being truthful. As anticipated, members were not able to make accurate conclusions. When it came to rating the degree of the depicted feeling, members were more exact in rating negative than positive, passionate appearances. This discovery stresses the possibility that it is more natural for people to lie about a negative feeling.

The second examination included a more significant number of members, more video parts, and a more extensive arrangement of passionate expressions from the recorded appearances. The negative feelings scale included things that the creators accepted would be significant to trickery, such as lament, blame, misery, outrage, and stress. These discoveries affirmed those of the main examination, demonstrating that members couldn't tell whether the general population in the recordings were lying or not, but instead could rate whether the general population in the tapes were feeling happy or angry.

In representing this impact, the creators come back to the possibility that maybe individuals are not precisely great at spotting a lie when it includes a negative feeling. It is likewise conceivable, however, that eyewitnesses changed their mindset when they're seeing the feelings of somebody who appears to be sad, hurt, or sorry. It's notable that individuals are better at making subjective decisions when they're in a terrible state of mind. When seeing somebody who appears to be miserable, compassion sets in, and you feel awful too. By then, you'll be ready to pass judgment on the subtleties of what somebody is feeling. How might you use this information to increase your advantage when you're trying to spot if somebody is truthful? Begin by checking whether you can understand which feelings the person is going through. Try and get an idea of the feeling you think the person is having through his words, if the feelings being communicated are sure, odds are, you won't make an accurate judgment. Instead, turn the discussion to increasingly pessimistic encounters, and after that see whether you think the person is telling the truth.

Difference between lying and deception

Our way of life makes an unusual similarity between lie and deceit. Accordingly, we have different sentiments about both ideas. One is thought of as "wrong," while the other is to a great extent endured.

To lie is to put forth a false expression with the goal to cheat, at the end of the day, lying is all about saying something that isn't valid. To deceive, on the other hand, is "to make someone accept what is false or invalid." In both cases, the victim believes something that isn't valid.

Lying is a type of trickery, while deception does not generally include lying.

The main difference between lying and deception can be found in the detail. Did you state something that isn't valid? It's safe to say that at that point, you lied. In any case, if you suggest something that wasn't valid, you didn't lie.

Deception techniques

The "Land of Is" Technique

Most questions need a yes or no answer. At the point when someone doesn't have any desire to answer yes or no, they regularly go to what is known as the Land of Is. The Land of Is can be known as the thin line between truth and deception. The Land of Is comprises of misleading statements, suspicions, and verbal judo. The vast majority need to come clean, so they put forth an attempt to twist the facts to keep up with the lies without letting it be known. People always end up in the Land of Is, and they never know it.

To test people to spot if they are lying, ask a yes or no question. On the off chance that they fail to answer yes or no, a warning should spring up. After somebody gives a tangled response to a question, ask once more. If the person fails to reply with a yes or no, there is a chance that the person is trying to deceive you.

The "Well" Answer

If you ask somebody a yes or no question, and you get an answer that starts with "Well," there is a chance that person is telling a lie. At the point when a person answers with "Well," it shows that the person is going to give an answer he thinks you are not anticipating.

How to be of Deceptive at Work

Building trust at work can be a tricky thing. With co-workers, your boss, and the people you just meet. There are very distinct signs to tell for sure though if someone at the office or in your work environment is deceitful. Here are some common behavior traits:

- **Morphing stories**

Someone who exaggerates or underestimates their stories is someone that is trying to hide something. For example, if you hear someone tell the same story, but the details are different each time. This someone is trying to hide that they weren't really sick that day. Or they are not so good at what they keep bragging that they are about.

- **Gossiper**

When someone gossips in the office about another person, you can be sure that you are their next target. This person makes it evident that they cannot be trusted, as it is a breach of privacy. When you see this happening either leave the office or continue to listen so you can learn how to "gossip" better. Learn what not to do and figure out just how to be discreet when telling secrets. Try out of the office for example.

- **A prominent flake.**

Ever been around someone who makes promises they don't keep? Or say things they don't act upon? This is a flake. If you want to be a better deceptionist than this person, maybe renege a couple of times. Remember, the goal is to gain trust so you can form a bond. Once the bond is formed, your excuses and flaking won't seem to be that big of a deal as they are under your spell.

- **Name dropper**

We all have been around that colleague who likes to blame specific people that may or may not have had anything to do with a situation. This is name dropping. To be good at this, get people hyped about a scenario or situation and then name the "who shall not be named" making it clear you would never drop names of others because it's "rude." Knowing full well, that is precisely what you are doing. Not only will people succumb to wanting to know more, but they will also fall for the demise you're trying to create. Making others think you are a good person will make them become drawn to you. Secrets are not made to be mentioned. Including yours.

Chapter 9
Hypnotism Utilization

Hypnosis is a cooperative interaction (or supposed to be a cooperative interaction) in which the participant responds to being entranced by the hypnotist. Hypnotism is used for all aspects of life. It is a form of getting into the mind, taking out the bad and replacing it with good. Or the other way around if you have dark intentions. Hypnosis is proven to reduce signs of anxiety and pain in patients with these illnesses.

The Four Stages of Hypnosis

Stage 1: Absorb Attention

This involves an attack on personality, which involves ideas like, "You are not who you think you are," a deliberate assault on the character or inner self of the victim. The operator denies everything that makes the identity of the person with statements like, "You are not a warrior." "You are not a man," and, "You are not guarding opportunity." To absorb the attention of the victim, the brainwasher draws them in using their tonality, their physiology, and their reputation to ensure the hypnosis is successful.

Stage 2: Bypass the Critical Faculty

The critical faculty is the part of the mind that uses logic and reasoning. If you have watched or read something that confuses you, and you are sure that what you are imagining cannot be possible, this is critical faculty. The operator tries to bypass this so that the victim can respond in an unconscious state. However, if the client feels threatened in any way through the process, the critical faculty will switch back on resulting in breaking the trance.

Stage 3: Activate an Unconscious Response

An unconscious response is that of a person communicating on a level of unawareness. The victim is unaware that they are being hypnotized, and will have no recollection of what is happening or what has happened throughout the process. The offender will dive into the victim's mind and place or replace thoughts, beliefs, perceptions, and values of the victim by creating visualizations for the client.

Stage 4: Leading the Unconscious to the Desired Outcome

Once the victim has reached all three stages of the hypnotic state, hypnotic suggestions and metaphors can be used. Hypnotic suggestions are used in commands and can be used to create an immediate or posthypnosis effect. Metaphors are stories cautiously constructed to help the unconscious mind become resourceful.

The Outcome

When all four stages are completed successfully, the result in the client or victim becomes whatever the perpetrator has brainwashed, or hypnotized into their mind, resulting in either a positive outcome or a negative one, depending on who you are dealing with.

How Does Hypnosis Work

Don't listen to the stereotypical point of view about hypnotism. It does not consist of a guy swinging a pocket watch in front of your face while saying phrases in a monotone voice. The hypnotist's job is to serve as a coach or trainer to help the client become hypnotized. Hypnotism is a state characterized by focused attention, heightened sensibility, and vivid fantasies. While a person is in the hypnotic state, they may come off as sleep or zoned out. In actuality, they are in a state of super high awareness. Hypnotherapists use visualization and verbal repetition to induce the hypnotic state.

The purpose for hypnosis is to get an individual to open up their mind to what they have buried deeper than the surface. The hypnotic state allows people to explore painful thoughts, feelings, and memories that are rather hard for them to bare consciously. Hypnotism is a treatment for sufferers to get them to perceive things differently. There are two ways hypnosis is used, suggestion therapy and analysis.

Suggestion Therapy

The client will be able to respond better to suggestions. This helps them change their behaviors such as to quit smoking or nail-biting. Suggestion therapy is very helpful with people who suffer chronic pain by changing the way they perceive sensations.

Analysis

This approach is used on people that suffer from mood, PTSD, and anxiety disorders. The analysis gets the client to a relaxed state so the hypnotist can find the psychological root of the problem. Once the problem is revealed, it can be addressed in psychotherapy.

How to Hypnotize Someone

It is easy to hypnotize a willing patient because in reality, they are actually hypnotizing themselves which is known as self-hypnosis. Your job as the hypnotist is to guide them into a relaxed state to fall into a waking sleep. This method is one of the easiest because you need no experience and can be used on the willing. This is called the progressive relaxation method.

Step One: Prepare

1. Find a willing participant to practice on.

If your participant doesn't want to be hypnotized, this can make things very difficult. You must find someone who is willing and believes it will work. Do not try to hypnotize someone with a history of mental disorders. It can lead to unintended consequences for that person.

2. Choose a safe and quiet place.

The environment has to have a relaxing vibe, so your client will be able to relax. Set the mood. This consists of dimming the lights and having a nice smelling surrounding. Have them sit in a comfortable chair and remove any distractions. This could be things like the TV, or putting the dog outside and the kids to bed. It should be just the two of you together. Be aware that cell phones should be turned off, windows should be closed, and letting people know that you are busy and not to be bothered.

3. Explanations.

Let the participant know what to expect and make sure they know the consequences. Maybe do some research together before starting, so that there are no misconceptions. As we have seen on TV and other series, most people may think too much into the stereotypes of hypnotism. It is best to let your client know that these are mythical, tell them the facts. Let them know they are not asleep or unconscious, they are not under a spell, and they will not do anything they don't want to do.

Step Two: Induce the Tranced State

1. Communicate in a low, slow, soothing voice.

Take your time when vocalizing to the participant. Your voice has to be smooth and calm. Draw out your sentences being careful not to put emphasis on them. When you are in the process of relaxing the participant, imagine you are trying to calm a frightened or worried person. It is best to keep a steady tone throughout the entire process.

Some words to start with can be, "Let my words settle you and take the suggestions as you wish," "You are safe. Everything is peaceful. Please sink into your chair and relax," "Your eyes are feeling heavy. Let your body relax. Listen to my body being aware of your muscles as you become more relaxed," and, "You are in complete control. Accept the suggestions given that only you are willing to benefit from."

2. Ask them to breathe deeply and slowly.

Using the same tone and concentration, ask them to breathe through their nose and out through their mouths. Ask them to pay attention to which part of the body they feel most of the oxygen coming from. It's like teaching them step by step how to breathe and focus their minds on just breathing. Let them know this is their only obligation, to just breathe. Make it important that the surroundings are calm and safe, and if their mind wanders to bring their attention back to the breath.

3. Focus their gaze.

Ask them to open their eyes if they are closed, unless they want to keep them closed, and focus on something. It can be your forehead, or something dimly lit. Once they have fixated on an object, ask them to focus intensely on this object, not looking away. Also, let them know it is okay to keep their eyes closed. If you notice that they are struggling to keep their eyes still, give them guidance, telling them to focus on something specific.

4. Get them to relax every inch of their body.

Once you notice your participant is calm and relaxed. Remind them to continue to breathe slowly. Now it is time to ask them to relax their toes and feet. Once they have done this carefully taking in a breath after relaxing their feet, move to the next muscle group. Ask them to relax their legs and calves, to their stomach, chest and back, and next to their arms and hands. Finally, ask them to relax the muscles on their shoulders, neck, and head. Take as much time as you need, and let them know they can take time as well. It is important not to rush.

5. Calm them further.

Make your voice repetitive at this stage. Tell them that with every word you whisper they are slowly sinking deeper and deeper into relaxation. Make it known that they are staying completely aware, yet completely relaxed. Reassure them that they are safe and then repeat the words "You are sinking deeper into relaxation now." If you notice their eyes are darting or they are subtly fidgeting, just focus their attention back to their breath. Reteach them to breathe slowly and deeply.

6. Visually create the relaxation staircase.

Tell your participant to picture a staircase that has ten steps. Tell them that with each step they walk down, their body gets lighter and their tension becomes no more. With every step down the stairs, they are taking in another deep breath. The goal is when they reach the bottom they are to be in full subconscious mode.

Step Three: Using Hypnosis to Help

1. Understand that tricking someone in this state usually doesn't work and is a trust violation.

Most people will remember their experience and be upset if you try to fool them. If you don't know what you are doing, then your good intentions can lead to bad results. The goal is to help your participant in letting go of their problems and life stresses.

2. Ask them to imagine solutions to their current problems.

Instead of telling the participant what to do or think, ask them to solve their own problems. Do this by telling them to imagine what their life is like in ten years from now, five years from now, a year from now and finally, a week from now. Ask them to picture all their problems and stresses that they are dealing with and then ask them to find the solution. Say things like, "What does success look like for you?" "How do you get there?" and "What do you want most from now to a month from now?" Ask them simple questions, but spin it positively.

3. Know that hypnosis is used for a variety of afflictions.

It is good to keep in your own mind that you are not a professional, and you won't be able to solve their issues. Understand the fact that hypnosis has been used for addiction, pain relief, phobias, self-esteem issues, and others. Unless guided by a hypnotist, you should stick to the basics. Ask the individual to imagine a day without smoking. Whatever they suffer from the most, ask them to picture a life with or without it to help them see there is a benefit.

Final Step Four: Ending the Session:

1. **Slowly take them out of this state.**

The last thing you want to do is alarm them out of the relaxation. Tell them the session is finished and to listen carefully to the instructions on how to come back. Let them know they are becoming aware of their surroundings. Ask your client to walk back up the stairs, back to where they came from. Once at the top of the stairs ask them to listen to what is around them, say they can move their toes and fingers. Finally, make them aware that once you count to five they can open their eyes and they will be fully alert. Then count to five slowly.

2. **Discuss the hypnosis.**

Go over what it was like for them so you can gain insight on how to improve. Ask them how they felt, and what they went through. Ask them what they enjoyed and did not enjoy. If they don't feel like talking, it is okay to give them time to talk about it later.

Chapter 10
Dark Seduction Psychology

Seduction is a process in which a person deliberately entices another person to get what they want in a sexual manner. Someone seduces another person because they want a relationship, to lead astray, to feel righteous. An offender can use seduction to corrupt or persuade sexual activity for a pleasurable benefit. Strategies include almost all of what we have learned in this book, such as nonverbal communication (NLP), deception, persuasion, short-term behavioral tactics, and enticing body language. If seduction is used negatively, it involves temptation and enticement to lead someone astray into a behavioral choice they wouldn't have made if they weren't in sexual arousal.

The Techniques Used in Dark Seduction

Sometimes, seduction has nothing to do with sex, but it's the game surrounding temptation. It's getting someone to become aroused for the sake of having their minds want what the offender wants. Seduction is another meaning for anticipation. Someone can be anticipated for anything such as a vacation or getting a new pet. It's the desire behind the temptation that has people searching and exploring their needs to get what they want. Continue reading for some tactics on how to use seduction negatively.

- **Choose the right victim.**

As explained throughout this book, you have now learned how to get to know someone thoroughly. Choosing someone who is susceptible to your charms is the best victim. This type of person has to be isolated, or unhappy and can easily be enticed into doing as you please. The perfect victim is someone who can be chased because your seductive measures will seem more natural and dynamic.

- **Create a sense of security—falsely.**

The offender should begin to seduce indirectly so that the target gradually becomes aware of you. If the perpetrator is direct too early, they risk stirring up resistance that will become impossible to get lower. It is best to approach the victim precariously through a third-party moving from friend to lover with their target. Once the victim feels secure and that they can trust you, that is when you strike.

- **Send mixed signals.**

Once the victim is aware and intrigued by you, you need to stimulate their interest before they move their attention elsewhere. Sending mixed messages like being harsh, then soft—both spiritual and earthly, innocent and cunning. The reason for this technique is because mixed signals can lead to the depth of a person. With wisdom comes intrigue and fascination. The target will be confused yet want to know more. To get the best result for this, you must create power by hinting at something contradictory within yourself.

- **Appear to be an object of desire.**

If you have attracted interest beyond other people, then you are most likely going to attract your target. People who fail to draw the attention of others fail in the temptation process. Create an aura of desirability to achieve the goal of attraction. If you are a trendsetter or the focus of attention, many people will want to "win" you over and take you away from the crowd of admirers.

- **Create a need—mix anxiety and discontentment.**

If you are trying to seduce a perfectly satisfied person, it will not work. To get the target to anticipate temptation with you, they must be tense and unrested. If they are on the brink of this or can be easily manipulated, you must instill feelings of discontent in them. Pain and anxiety are the perfect preconditions to pleasure.

- **Master insinuation**

If your target feels dissatisfied and relies on you to meet their attention, then this is crucial to seducing them. If you are too obvious in your tricks, then you will be left with no victim as they will run from you. Insinuation consists of planting a seed inside the mind of the target. So to drop a hint, then days later they have it appear as if it was their idea is how insinuation works best. To do this, the offender says something bold followed by a retraction and an apology, evasive comments, and small talk combined with alluring glances.

- **Create temptation.**

By creating temptation, you can easily lure your victim into your trap. Awake the desire in your targets so that they want more, and they cannot control themselves. Find their weakness and exploit it. Show them their fantasies can come to life. Stimulate curiosity stronger than doubt and anxiety that goes with the unknown.

- **Keep them guessing.**

If you make it known what to expect from you, then the spell will be broken. By creating suspense, it keeps the victim on point, always guessing whats next. This keeps them intrigued and wanting more. People like to be spontaneous, whether they like to admit that or not, so surprising them will give them a sense of spontaneity. Just as you are heading one way, change direction giving the victim thrill and excitement.

- **Pay attention to detail.**

Thoughtful gifts made just for them, clothes, jewelry, or anything designed to please them will have them mesmerized by you. If you shower them with the attention they don't normally get, then they will continue to stay your prize. Doing this shows them that you pay attention to their needs and give them what they want. Little do they know it's a setup for getting what you so desire.

- **Poeticize your presence.**

When an offender leaves their victim alone for too long, their victim will become distant. If a target thinks their offender is not around, the game is over. The trick is to remain elusive. Create memories through objects. Associate yourself with images and nonverbal actions. That way when the victim lives their lives when the perpetrator is busy, the victim can envelop the offender in their fantasies when they think or see something that reminds them of their person.

- **Disarm through weaknesses and vulnerability.**

Put the shoe on the other foot. Your perfect target is weak and vulnerable. Up to this point they are enthralled by you. It's time to turn the tables. You need to strategize how you portray your weaknesses and vulnerabilities. This is to make them feel superior like they want to help you and engage with your emotions. This will also make them feel like you are opening up and your actions will seem more natural. Play the victim, then transform the subject's sympathy into love.

- **Mix pleasure with pain.**

The worst thing someone can do while trying to seduce is to be too kind. If the offender works too hard, they will come off as insecure and monotonous. When things start to get good, inflict the target with pain. Make them feel guilty and create the illusion of a breakup. When they are feeling helpless and cry out for the need of you again, return to being nice and you will have them. The lower the blows, the higher the make-up will be. To excite the seduction, create fear.

By becoming what someone needs at the time, and then forcing a whirlwind of distraction, confusion, the ups, and the downs, you will become their biggest fantasy. Careful not to overdo anything, and plan out your moves strategically. The minute someone feels they are being played, it's game over.

Why People Use Seduction

People use seductions for many reasons such as getting ahead in their career, moving to the next stage in a relationship and getting something they want for a deal. Manipulators use seduction for personal benefits and pleasure. Seduction is something that can be dangerous, or very harmless. The choice is yours. Here is what you will need to contain seduction successfully.

- **Desire**

Awakening the desire, in the target of interest is key to temptation. Desire is much like ambition. Go after what you want because you want it so badly. Overcoming the fear of failure will help you become successful in fulfilling this trait. The idea of desire is to keep the anticipation of what's next to come. The answer is never a no, but a possible yes, or a maybe. Keep the victim guessing leaving them wanting more.

Trigger emotional buttons in people, and you will master the art of seduction.

- **Confidence**

You can't seduce someone if you don't have the confidence to know you can. So in short, without confidence comes no temptation. The key to confidence is trusting yourself. If you trust yourself, then you can trust that there are lots to love about you. If you like yourself, then insecurities can't get in your head. Confident people's aura shows that they are happy to be who they are. Hence, confident people will usually get what they want. Fake it until you make it is often what is said. This means if you are not something that you want to be, fake it and it shall become real over time.

- **Arousal**

Find out what makes someone vulnerable and play on that emotion. This will awaken their arousal. The goal is to get in touch with your skills. What makes you so intriguing? When you can answer this for yourself, you will be able to show this answer to someone else. Thus, they will lust you, and you will have succeeded in opening their arousal.

Master these three elements, and you will become the master charmer. When you build a connection with people, you can exploit their resources and affection to get what you want in the end. When you achieve the role in temptation, then you will be more confident. Confidence leads to greater success through life. See where I am going with this?

Chapter 11

Psychological Warfare

Psychological Warfare is the planned tactical use of publicity, threats, and other noncombat techniques during wars, or periods of conflict. The purpose was to mislead, intimidate, demoralize, or influence the behavior and thoughts of the enemy. To be successful in the army's objectives, the planners of psychological warfare (PSYWAR) campaigns, they gained complete knowledge of the enemy's beliefs, likes and dislikes, strengths and weaknesses, and vulnerabilities. This was so they could win the war.

Other names for PSYWAR are MISO, PSYOP (psychological operations), "hearts and minds," and propaganda. Various techniques are used to stimulate confessions or reinforce attitudes and behaviors to the originator's objectives. Target audiences are not just limited to soldiers, but governments, companies, groups, and individuals.

In early psychological warfare, soldiers would beat their swords against their shields as a sign to threaten or instill fear in their opponents. In the 525 BC Battle of Peluseium, Persian forces would hold cats hostage to gain leverage over the Egyptians because of the religious beliefs they had—not to harm cats. In the thirteenth century AD, the Mongolian Empire leader made his troops carry three lit torches at a time as a means to make his army look bigger. To frighten villagers, the Mongol armies would catapult human heads over village walls.

In modern psychological warfare, during World War I, technological advances made it easier for government systems to distribute propaganda through mass-circulation newspapers. During World War II, Hitler's rise to power was driven by propaganda in Germany, designed to discredit his political opponents. His angry speeches compiled national pride while convincing villagers to blame others for Germany's self-induced economic problems.

Techniques and Methods

Psychological Warfare is a method that uses fear and uncertainty to break down the mental and emotional well-being of an opponent. Here is a list of techniques that are used:

1. News Outlets

The news is an information panel that almost everyone sees or reads. The press can run whatever information it chooses, whether it's government-run or independently owned. A population could be tainted or brainwashed by paying attention to the news. Most of the time the story happens to be correct, and so it is a viable source people will listen to.

2. Threats

Whether they be empty threats or actual—threats of violence, restriction of freedom, and control—is made to instill fear in people or organizations. Constant warnings can damage a group or individuals psychological state resulting in anxiety and terror.

3. Leaflets

Leaflets are pieces of paper dropped by air forces over war territories that have manipulative messages or pictures written on them. The goal is to get the opponent to surrender or fight the political event taking place.

4. Objects

Objects are souvenirs like T-shirts, posters, hats, pins, and so on. This is another effective way to get a message or point across. The objects can become symbols for more prominent correspondence regarding politics, beliefs, religious philosophies, etc. They are used for worship and promotion.

5. False Flag

A false flag is an empty threat or a message that consists of a lie to instill concern or dread in people. The blame is put on a different organization to gain control and shift attention.

6. Media

Media is a discreet way to get in our head through subliminal messages. Films, music, and books are tools for psychological warfare. The media can form a new perspective and put ideas in the minds of the population.

7. Demoralization

Demoralization consists of direct transmission through publications or radio, books, and pamphlets, delivery systems like airplane drops, smuggling, and deception. Demoralization in the context of PSYWAR is the objective to weaken morale among enemy combatants. This encourages the opponent to retreat, surrender, or fight rather than defeating them on the battlefield.

Chapter 12

Case Studies

Some case studies in this chapter are considered wrong and ruthless. Before reading or listening, be advised that some of the content matter may be offensive or derogative. These are dark examples of experiments used by psychologists and scientists. There are many more case studies than what is written here, but these are to get you to understand the different ways dark psychology has come about. Many of these experiments have a hidden meaning regardless of the intention of the projects. Enjoy.

Wild Boy of Aveyron

The "Wild Boy of Aveyron" named Victor lived in the forest of Aveyron for several years in the 1800s. He was age eleven or twelve. After he had been spotted leaving the forest of Aveyron, psychologists and philosophers studied him naming him the "natural experiment."

This is how the question nature versus nurture came to life. When Victor was brought into civilization, he was dirty and tousled. Food was something that largely motivated him. When he was transported to Paris and Itard, the cities began a mission to teach the boy how to socialize and become a part of society. The program was slightly successful, but not quite. Victor never learned to speak fluently, but he learned how to dress and use the washroom. He learned how to write and acquired basic comprehension. Scientists will never know his background but have theories revolving around autism. Autism expert Uta Frith believed that Victor got abandoned because he may have had autism. Because of this case, the boy has been an inspiration throughout history. A 2004 novel called The Wild Boy was published and was dramatized in the 1970 French film called The Wild Child.

H. M.

Henry Molaison died in 2008, gocs by H. M. to protect his privacy to the public. He had severe amnesia as age twenty-seven after having brain surgery for treatment from epilepsy. Over 100 psychologists and neurologists studied him and had been mentioned in twelve thousand or more journal articles. Molaison's surgery involved removing a large part of the hippocampus part of the brain on both sides. The result was that he lost almost all of his long-term memory. Considering researchers and scientists studied that only the cerebral cortex was to blame for memory loss, this brain surgery was quite the popular focus. Molaison's brain was carefully sliced and preserved which is now turned into a 3-D digital atlas.

Anna O.

Anna O. is a pseudonym for Bertha Pappenheim, who died in 1936 age seventy-seven. She was a German Jewish feminist and social worker. As Anna O, she is known as one of the first patients ever to undergo psychoanalysis, and her case inspired Freud's thoughts on mental illness. Joseph Breuer, a psychoanalyst, was brought to her house in Vienna, where he witnesses her lying in her bed entirely paralyzed. Some symptoms she had experienced was hallucinations, personality changes, and rambling speech, in which doctors found no physical cause. Breuer visited her almost every day for eighteen months and talked to her. They spoke of her thoughts and feelings, including her grief for her father, and what seemed to be the most interesting was that the more she talked, the more her symptoms would fade. Researchers had named this the "talking cure," first ever instances revolving psychoanalysis. In the later days of Pappenheim's life, she had become a productive writer which she included authoring stories, plays, and translation. She founded social clubs for Jewish women and the German Federation of Jewish Women. She also worked in orphanages.

Little Albert

Little Albert was the nickname for John Watson; a behaviorist psychologist had given to an eleven-month-old baby. John Watson alongside his fiancé Rosalind Rayner deliberately attempted to instill specific fears in the child through a process called conditioning. The results were documented in 1920 and had become notorious for being the most unethical procedure ever done. A few years later, an academic quarrel had erupted over Little Albert's true identity. A group led by Hall Beck confirmed in 2011 that Little Albert's real name was Douglas Meritte, the son of a wet nurse (a woman employed to breastfeed another woman's child) at John Hopkins University—where Watson and his fiancé were based. Based on this knowledge, that would mean sadly that Little Albert died at the age of six because of a condition called hydrocephalus (fluid in the brain). However, this knowledge was challenged by a different group led by Russel Powell. Their theory was that Little Albert actual name was William A Barger (recorded in his medical files as Albert Barger) the son of a different wet nurse. Later in the year 2015, textbook writer confirmed that the second theory was more credible. If this is true, that would mean that Little Albert died at age eighty-seven in 2007.

Chris Sizemore

Chris Sizemore is most famous for having been diagnosed with multiple personality disorder, known today as a dissociative identity disorder. Sizemore's alter egos names were Eve White, Eve Black, Jane, and multiple others. Sizemore expressed these personalities as a coping mechanism for her traumatic childhood. She said she had witnessed her man being beaten and saw a man sawn in half. Later in Sizemore's life, she mentioned that her alter egos were combined into one. She had explained that Eve White was the mother of her first child and that Eve White was married to her husband and she wasn't. Later, her story was turned into a movie in 1957 called The Three Faces of Eve. In 1977, Sizemore published her autobiography called I'm Eve, and in 2009, she appeared on the BBC's Hard Talk interview series.

David Reimer

Reimer lost his penis in a circumcision operation when he was eight months old. His parents were advised by a psychologist John Money to raise Reimer as a girl, so his parents renamed him Brenda. They set up plans and further surgery to get him to go through hormone treatment to assist a gender reassignment. The assignment was problematic because of Reimer's boyish personality and found out the truth about himself at age fourteen. Later, he campaigned against other children with genital injuries being gender reassigned the same way he had been. His story was turned into a book named As Nature Made Him: The Boy Who Was Raised as a Girl by John Colapinto. He is also the subject of two BBC horizon documentaries. Unfortunately, Reimer killed himself when he was thirty-eight years old in 2004.

Emma Eckstein

Sigmund Freud decided to use Eckstein for various experiments after she had asked him for help with stomach ailments and slight depression. Freud told Eckstein that she was being treated for hysteria and excessive masturbation repetitively. At that time, these two habits were known as mental illness. Freud gave

Emma cocaine, and a local anesthetic before the inside of her nose was cauterized—a disastrous treatment. He continued to treat her with this for three years, and no one knows what his intentions were to this day.

Electroshock Therapy on Children

Dr. Lauretta Bender of the Creedmore Hospital in New York chose over one hundred young children to use electroshock therapy on based on her theoretic beliefs. Bender made her patients sit in front of a large group and applied pressure to their foreheads. Any child who slightly cringed or moved because of the pressure was thought to have early signs of schizophrenia. Bender believed electroshock therapy was the only treatment to solve this social issue. Her peers confirmed that they thought she had never shown sympathy for the children in her care. The youngest child to be worked on was three years old.

The Monster Study

In 1939, twenty-two orphans living in Davenport, Iowa, became test subjects of a couple named Wendell Johnson and Mary Tudor. The study consisted of speech impediments and stuttering. The children were split in half, into two groups. One group received positive speech therapy and were praised consistently on their speech. The other group received negative speech therapy. This included being belittled for any speech imperfection and violent consequences. The conclusion of the study was the children in the second, negative group developed speech problems throughout their lives and had never had imperfections before the experiment. The experiment was never published because Johnson and Tudor feared the comparisons people would believe of human experiments among the Nazis.

Project MK-Ultra

Project MK-Ultra was an experiment involving violent torture such as giving subject's mind-altering drugs, sensory deprivation, verbal and sexual abuse, extreme isolation and hypnosis. This experiment was meant to figure out the best ways to manipulate the mental states of American citizens. The project was funded and sponsored by the CIA and could find these experiments being done at prisons, hospitals, and universities. Luckily, Congress shut down Project MK-Ultra later in the year 1973. This experiment went on for twenty years starting in 1953.

The Monkey Drug Trials

A research facility began an unethical experiment on monkeys in 1969. They wanted to test the effects of drug addiction, so they trained a large number of monkeys on how to inject themselves with needles. The various drugs were morphine, alcohol, cocaine, nicotine, codeine, and amphetamines. When the monkeys learned how to inject themselves, they were left in a room with a significant supply of drugs lying around. The monkey went haywire. Their acts consisted of breaking limbs to escape the lab, pulling hair from a specific part of their bodies, and others mixed a bunch of drugs in which they died shortly after.

Facial Expressions Experiment

Carney Landis began an experiment to study common facial expression. He wanted to know if everyone had the same facial expression based on what they saw. The facial expressions he wanted to experiment with were happiness, shock, and disgust. To conduct his experiment, Landis recruited many participants and painted their facial lines black. He then exposed his participants to images and videos like pornography, ammonia, touching reptiles, and beheading rats. Once the participants had an expression, he would snap their photograph to save for his results. This happened in 1924.

Bobo Doll Experiment

In the 1960s, psychologist Albert Bandura wanted to test how children learn behaviors based on their influences. Bandura got a large doll named Bobo and had a percentage of seventy-two primary-aged children watch adults violently beat this doll. Then he left the children in a room alone with Bobo and observed what they would do. A large number of children also began to abuse the doll quite violently. Bandura repeated this experiment twice, and the results were the same.

Racism among Elementary School Students

Jane Elliott, a schoolteacher, experimented with her student to teach them about racism. Many outsiders judged her publicly for her teaching methods, and others had an issue with the fact that she was exposing white children to such measures. The experiment was successful and was perhaps a life lesson for all the students. In 1968, Martin Luther King Jr. had been assassinated, so while Elliott tried to explain racism to her children, she asked the students with blue eyes to go to one side of the room while the kids with brown stayed on the other side. The kids with blue eyes, she treated as a superior group and cited fake scientific studies claiming those with blue eyes were better. A week later, she switched groups and provided the same tactic with the ones with brown eyes. Elliott received public backlash because of this. But the method got the point across, and some may consider her a hero.

Conclusion

Finally, dark psychology will never disappoint when employed positively. If you got to the end of this book, there is no way back. Armed with this strength of knowledge, you should be ready to put dark art skills in practice at the office, in church, or at home in your relationships.

Simply follow the techniques discussed in the book, and you can easily persuade anyone. The application of dark psychology is a two-way street; you can stop the smooth criminal in their tracks because it now takes just a second to spot this deceptive person weaving their way into your mind and soul through peddling lies. Or you can choose to become the predator weaving your way into other people's lives.

The myths that have stood for ages have been shattered in this book; and this book clearly explains the skills used in the dark arts that the public previously thought was magic. Hypnotism, for instance, is a misunderstood science, but its benefits are numerous, and its utility can save lives.

The dark traits discussed here are living examples that we experience in everyday life and not mere illusions in a movie.

You can rest easy and cast your fears and doubts of dark psychology and begin the journey to becoming a better and skilled dark psychologist. Don't keep waiting anymore. Go ahead, put your skills into practice and implement what you have learnt.

www.ingramcontent.com/pod-product-compliance
Lightning Source LLC
Chambersburg PA
CBHW020256030426
42336CB00010B/786